FAMILIES AGAINST SOCIETY

Volume 88, Sage Library of Social Research

Sage Library of Social Research

FAMILIES AGAINST SOCIETY

A Study of Reactions to Children with Birth Defects

ROSALYN BENJAMIN DARLING

Foreword by JETSE SPREY

Volume 88
SAGE LIBRARY OF
SOCIAL RESEARCH

 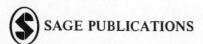 

SAGE PUBLICATIONS   Beverly Hills   London

For information address:

SAGE Publications, Inc.
275 South Beverly Drive
Beverly Hills, California
90212

SAGE Publications Ltd
28 Banner Street
London EC1Y 8QE
England

Printed in the United States of America

Library of Congress Cataloging in Publication Data
Darling, Rosalyn Benjamin.
    Families against Society
    (Sage library of social research; v. 88)
    Bibliography: p.
    1. Handicapped children—United States—Family relationships. 2. Abnormalities, Human—Psychological aspects.
    3. Abnormalities, Human—Social aspects.
I. Title.
HV888.5.D37   362.7'8   79-14148
ISBN 0-8039-1285-4
ISBN 0-8039-1286-2 pbk.

FIRST PRINTING

CONTENTS

LIST OF TABLES AND DIAGRAMS

FOREWORD

One of the nostalgic assumptions many people — sociologists and laypersons alike — still hold is that families and their communities are existing under conditions of mutual interdependence and cooperation. Presumably, families provide community members with a much needed refuge from the hardships of everyday social life. The community, in its turn, through its major social institutions, helps families in their continuing struggle for survival. Most obvious, among such helping institutions, are the school system, institutional medicine, the juvenile court system, and a range of other social welfare associations, each of which is staffed, in its own way, by a host of well-trained, benevolent, and highly motivated professionals. So the story goes. Of course, there are problems, but they are most often defined in strictly financial terms, thereby making solutions appear simple: more money is needed to hire more professionals. We find this premise, and its implicit rationale, still firmly entrenched in much of our current family and social work literature.

During recent years, however, those of us who have attempted to understand crisis management in families have become aware that the above approach is overly simplistic and increasingly invalid. Families, for example, do not always share the views of school boards, liberal judges, parole officers, and even physicians with regard to the well-being of their offspring. Some of these disputes seem related to social class. Others may reflect differing ethnic and political orientations, but these are the relatively simple cases. Still others, in my view, relate to the widening gap between families and the ever-growing power of our caring institutional support systems. To the latter helping somehow seems to demand rendering the recipients of their support helpless in return. Caring becomes an end in itself, rather than a means to achieve a broader goal.

A further complicating factor is that the increasing inability of most social institutions to perform their functions properly has led to the rediscovery of the family as a potential "adjunct" in providing "expert" care to its own members. Unfortunately, such care would have to be delivered under the strict guidance, or tutelage, of the helping organization's administrators and professionals. In the realm of medical care, for example, we do observe the recent "discovery" that some chronic patients — but not all — really are better off living, and dying at home. However, deciding *who* should be at home, or should be allowed to live or die, firmly remains in the hands of the representatives of institutionalized medicine. There is something to be said for this, but it is naive to assume that medical judgments in this so important realm of a family's existence always will be acceptable. Furthermore, it is becoming clear that those hospital administrators, physicians, or public health nurses who are empowered to make decisions which drastically affect the lives of family members, often know very little about the ways in which contemporary families function. On the contrary, their ideas about the availability and limitations of familial resources frequently are outdated, naive, and unrealistic.

It is in this context that Dr. Darling's book makes a valuable contribution to our understanding of what parents necessarily must cope with after the birth of a severely disabled child, and of how they must negotiate with persons in an institutonal environment who may not share their private goals and aspirations, but on whom they must depend for support. Many of the parents included in this book did indeed confront society, because they decided to follow their own counsel, rather than that of their medical and other advisors. They rejected the judgment that their severely disabled children should not be cared for at home. They also disagreed with the premise that their child might be better off not being alive at all.

I am not arguing that — objectively, or morally speaking — the decisions made by *all* Dr. Darling's subjects were wise ones. That is not the immediate issue here. Many parents in the sample were quite poorly prepared for the enormity of the responsibility which was so suddenly thrust upon them. Perhaps some should have selected different options. The fact is that they chose *not* to do so, and consequently had to face the hostility, or indifference of many of those to whom they had to turn to for assistance. We see parents who have to shop for a pediatrician willing to take their child as a patient, or, later, for a school inclined to consider their son or daughter educable. They, and their children, seemed guilty till proven innocent, while counsel for the defense often was hard to find.

Dr. Darling's study is exploratory. As such, it is not designed to provide a great many definitive answers. Rather, it raises a host of significant questions. Furthermore, it offers valuable insights into the topic of crisis management in ordinary families. It reveals how spouses do manage to adjust previously held high parental expectations to a reality of a quite different nature.

Finally, *Families against Society*, clearly shows our current inability — socially as well as culturally — to deal with life as a "quality" rather than a mere "quantity" in an age in which, biologically speaking, mere survival no longer is the main issue. It is apparent also, that when our legal and moral experts fail to arrive at any consensus — let alone a policy for action — it is, as always, the family which must confront and deal with such questions of life, death, and the quality of its collective survival.

— Jetse Sprey,
Case Western Reserve University,
Cleveland, Ohio.

PREFACE

In the three years since I began the research for this monograph, I have been gratified by many positive responses I have received from physicians, human services professionals, parents, and students in a variety of fields. Clearly, the interest in a sociological perspective on birth defects is wide-ranging, and many are ready to accept a view that challenges the traditional, victim-blaming conception of birth defects as an individual problem of adjustment. As my research shows, the "problem" posed by a congenitally handicapped child is largely a social one. Highly "accepting" parents will continue to encounter numerous difficulties as long as society is not "accepting." In order to understand the situation of defective children and their parents, one *must* explore the interactional context of that situation. I certainly hope that further studies of the handicapped will be undertaken from this perspective.

I owe my own appreciation of the interactionist viewpoint mostly to Joseph F. Zygmunt, who, both as teacher and dissertation adviser at The University of Connecticut, broadened my knowledge and encouraged my interest in this area. The other members of my dissertation committee, Stan Ingman, Walter I. Wardwell, and Robert M. Greenstein, have also been very helpful and encouraging throughout the research process. The idea that originated the research for this book was suggested by Bob Greenstein. I am truly appreciative of his continuing support and cooperation, especially since his viewpoint, as a physician, sometimes differed from mine, as a sociologist.

I would also like to thank the staff at the genetic counseling service that provided access to the research population used in the study. The nurse-associate at the service generously shared her office and her time with me during the sample selection process.

More than anyone else involved in this book, I would like to thank my husband, Jon, whose support and encouragement enabled me to resume a career I had set aside for several years. My work is truly the result of his patience and understanding as a sociologist, husband, babysitter, and friend.

I would like to express my appreciation as well to the series editor, Jetse Sprey, and the National Council on Family Relations for their interest in cosponsoring this book. Jetse Sprey has made many good suggestions in the final editing, and I am very grateful for his help.

Finally, I want to thank the parents and pediatricians who participated in the research. They were all extremely generous with their time, candor, and courtesy. I only hope that I have not misrepresented any of their positions. The parents, especially, made this book possible. They welcomed me into their homes and shared some of their most private and personal thoughts and feelings with me. Although they must remain anonymous, they deserve any credit that is due for showing me what sociology is really all about.

For my mother, Lillian Benjamin,
my husband, Jon,
and my children, Eric and Seth

INTRODUCTION

Society does not value all of its members equally, and resources are consequently differentially distributed in the population. Those in disfavored positions do not necessarily accept, however, the judgment of others in society. The processes through which these disfavored individuals and groups come to acquire and implement their counterdefinitions should be of considerable interest to sociologists and social psychologists, particularly those concerned with social change. Studies of the adaptations achieved by these "deviant" members might also be of importance to policy makers and other societal representatives who evaluate existing social definitions and the consequent treatment these members receive from various "service" agencies.

One disfavored segment of the population that tends to have an especially high number of contacts with service agencies of a medical, social, and educational nature are the physically and mentally handicapped. In the case of congenital handicaps, the frequency of these contacts is highest during early childhood, when problems are first recognized. This study is concerned with the interactional adaptations of parents of children with severe birth defects. As the data to be presented will indicate, these parents often become frustrated by the lack of appropriate societal resources for, or interest in, the treatment of their children. They consequently come

to adopt a role I have called "parental entrepreneurship."[1]
My focus will be on the entrepreneurship role from a
"career" perspective (Becker, 1963), in terms of its development over time, as parents continue to interact in a sometimes
hostile society.

The original aim of the study differed somewhat from its
ultimate direction. In its first conception, the research was
designed to explore the questions, both moral and scientific,
of the quality of life of the severely handicapped. My interest
in this area arose as a result of a conversation with a geneticist
concerning the "right-to-life" of children with a grossly
disabling birth defect: myelomeningocele-hydrocephalus.
The defect involves a spinal lesion and an abnormal ac-
cumulation of fluid in the head, which, when left untreated,
generally results in early mortality. Survival chances can be
greatly increased through early surgical intervention.
However, survivors are likely to have a high degree of
physical impairment, including paralysis, deformity, and in-
continence, and, in some, cases, mental retardation as well.

A leading physician in the field has summarized the situation as follows:

> In summary, at the most 7% of those admitted have less than
> grossly crippling disabilities and may be considered to have a
> quality of life not inconsistent with self-respect, earning
> capacity, happiness and even marriage. The next 20% are also
> of normal intelligence and some may be able to earn their liv-
> ing in sheltered employment, but their lives are full of illness
> and operations. They are severely handicapped and are
> unlikely to live a full lifespan. They are at a risk of sudden
> death from shunt complications or are likely to die of renal
> failure at an early age. The next 14% are even more severely
> handicapped because they are retarded. They are unlikely to
> earn their living and their opportunities in life will be severely
> restricted. They will always be totally dependent on others.
> Fifty-nine percent of those admitted are dead (Lorber, 1971:
> 286).

As a result, Lorber advocates a policy of *selection* of cases to be treated, based on such physiological criteria as the degree of paralysis present at birth. The majority of cases, who are left untreated, receive only minimal nursing care until they die. While Lorber's selection policy has been adopted by many hospitals in Britain and the United States, its morality continues to be questioned (see, for example, Freeman, 1974). Although absolute questions about the right to life and death perhaps lie more within the philosophical than the sociological domain, important sociological issues are raised by such questions: How are decisions about life and death actually made in the everyday interactional situation of the hospital? What are the consequences of such decisions for those involved and for society as a whole? An exploration of such issues might, in turn, be useful to decision makers in arriving at or justifying their actions.

Thus, I was originally concerned with the sociological implications of medical decisions to withhold treatment in cases such as myelomeningocele-hydrocephalus. More specifically, I was interested in the quality of life of the severely handicapped, that is, those from whom medical treatment necessary for survival was *not* withheld. A finding that such survivors and their families participated in or even enjoyed ordinary social interaction might raise doubts about Lorber's purely physiological selection policy or other arguments for nontreatment.

The first problem of the study, then, became one of operationalizing "quality of life." From a vast array of sociological variables, I chose the concept of self-esteem as a heuristic starting-point. Because high self-esteem has been correlated with "success" in such diverse areas of life as school performance (Rosenberg, 1965; Coopersmith, 1967) and physical rehabilitation (Litman, 1962), I felt that the concept might also be an indicator, in some measure, of quality of life. If handicapped children acquire high self-esteem in spite of their handicaps, I reasoned, perhaps they should not be denied lifesaving treatment at birth.

My original expectation was that children with severe birth defects would in fact have low self-esteem. The basis for this anticipated finding was my familiarity with the literature on stigmatization. Goffman (1963) and others have convincingly presented the case of the detrimental effect of societal stigma on the handicapped and other "deviant" individuals. Conclusions derived from a review of the literature on the self-esteem of the physically and mentally handicapped were not so clear, however. Many disabled people in fact appear to have self-esteem levels that are not different from those of matched normal control groups (see, for example, Shelsky, 1957; Zunich and Ledwith, 1965; Krider, 1959) *in spite of* societal stigma.

My interest thus shifted from the question of whether or not the handicapped had high self-esteem to that of how various self-esteem levels were determined. I wondered how stigmatized individuals managed to see themselves favorably in an unfavorable social context. An understanding of the determinants of high self-esteem in such cases might be valuable to those charged with deciding whether a defective infant should live or die. Knowledge of "esteem-promoting" social conditions seemed to be at least as important as Lorber's physiological criteria for treatment.

A review of the literature on the determinants of self-esteem suggests that self-concept formation takes place largely through interaction in small, personalized "reference groups" within the larger society. In the case of children, the most important reference group is generally shown to be the family, especially the parents. Thus, if parents define their children positively, their children are likely to have high self-esteem, regardless of the views of anyone else in society. One might therefore expect that congenitally handicapped children with high self-esteem would have parents who accepted and approved of them.

My concern at this point, then, was to discover how parents came to define their disabled children either positively or negatively. As a result, I reviewed the literature on "parental acceptance" of physically and mentally handicapped children. Most of the literature consisted of studies, undertaken from a psychoanalytic perspective, that attempted to determine those parental traits that prevented the formation of guilt (see, for example, Zuk, 1962). A few studies (Voysey, 1975; Birenbaum, 1970) have been concerned with the interactional context within which parental definitions develop. Although Voysey has traced the mechanisms through which such definitions arise in the course of everyday interaction, she does not suggest a patterned sequence of definitional change. As a symbolic interactionist concerned with process, I became interested in the time element in definitional development. Discovering sequences or "careers" of parental acceptance thus became the first goal of my research.

The most satisfactory method of obtaining information about the interactional sequences involved in the defining process is probably the longitudinal study based on interviewing or observation. Ideally, parents might be interviewed and observed at the time of their child's birth and again at various intervals continuing through the child's adolescence. Such an approach would require a protracted period of study, which was not feasible in this case. As a result, I chose what I believed to be the next best method: interviewing in depth the parents of children ranging in age from birth to 19 years. The interviews were conducted from a life history perspective in order to obtain data on sequences of events.

After encountering difficulties in obtaining a sample from the myelomeningocele clinic of a local children's hospital, I broadened my focus somewhat to include other seriously disabling conditions in addition to myelomeningocele. I decided on two criteria necessary for a defect to be included in my sample: (1) the problem had to be readily apparent to a lay person looking at such a child (i.e., the child had to be "discredited" rather than "discreditable," in Goffman's [1963] terms) and (2) the problem had to be incapacitating to the point of restricting the child's participation in some ordinary social activities. I found a ready source of cases meeting these criteria in the files of the Genetic Counseling Service at a local university-affiliated health center.

The families of 25 children were randomly selected for study, and in most cases, both the mother and father of each child were interviewed in their homes. The interview lasted approximately two to five hours with any one parent and was recorded on tape. My approach in the interviews was similar to analytic induction (Robinson, 1951), in that I attempted to isolate a pattern or patterns common to all of the families. The initial guiding hypothesis, derived from symbolic interaction theory, was that parents who defined their children positively would have been immersed in reference groups that defined their children in an approving manner. Parents who defined their children negatively, on the other hand, were expected to have been exposed to reference groups that echoed or did not insulate them from societal stigma.

In addition to the interview, the parents were asked to complete a version of the Twenty Statements Test (Kuhn and McPartland, 1954), in which they were asked to describe their real and "ideal" children in both the present and the future. The test was intended as a further measure of parents' definitions of their children and as a check on the interview data.

As the study progressed, I realized I would have difficulty comparing parents who approved with those who disapproved of their children. Although the sample was randomly drawn, all of the parents, without exception, seemed to accept and love their children, (a finding possibly related to the inclusion of only intact families in the sample). The main source of this acceptance was interaction with the children themselves. Typically, families became closer after the birth of their handicapped child, sometimes to the exclusion of other friends and relatives. Generally, those who remained closely integrated in preexisting family and friendship networks found these relationships to be supportive. Others had become involved in new relationships, sometimes with other parents of handicapped children.

Although all of the families seemed to have accepted their children and to have found support for that acceptance, the large majority reported numerous difficulties in interacting within the larger society. Most had experienced some rejection by others, and by various "helping" professionals, especially physicians. Many of the parents had a considerable amount of experience with doctors because of their children's continuing medical problems. Although these interactions were frequent and of long duration, generally medical professionals did not become highly salient "significant others" for parents unless they were supportive of parents' definitions.

This finding led me to select a smaller sample of pediatricians for further study. I was interested in understanding their viewpoint on the treatment of seriously handicapped children and their parents. Patient-physician interaction seemed to be of a microcosm of the larger society, in which positive parental definitions might be challenged. I felt, therefore, that an understanding of this relationship might shed light on other parental interactions as well.

I interviewed 15 pediatricians at their offices. The sample consisted of doctors randomly selected from a list of area pediatricians, the specialists with whom parents are likely to have the most frequent and intense contacts. These interviews lasted approximately 45 minutes to an hour and focused on two problem areas that had been stressed by parents: the situation of informing families about their children's problems, and attitudes toward treating handicapped children in the doctor's everyday practice.

The pediatricians I interviewed varied considerably in their attitudes toward handicapped children and their parents. Many, however, made statements that supported the parents' contention that doctors do not enjoy working with their children and that they try to avoid such interactions as much as possible. The physicians' feelings in this area seemed to relate to their inability to "cure" such children's chronically disabling conditions. Some went so far as to take a "victim-blaming" stance, suggesting that parents who kept their seriously handicapped children at home rather than institutionalizing them should expect to have problems.

Countering such victim-blaming definitions had become a major concern of many of the parents I interviewed. Most had encountered such a perspective in dealing with educational, social, and psychological specialists in addition to medical professionals. Most parents reported having accepted professional control during a period following the birth of their child. However, most quickly became disenchanted with professional advice (or more commonly, the lack of advice) and moved into a phase I have called "seekership" (after Lofland and Stark, 1965), in which they search for alternative definitions of the situation and solutions to their child-rearing problems.

Eventually, parents either find desired solutions in the form of appropriate school programs and doctors who accept their children, or, they enter a protracted period of "crusadership." The entrepreneurial crusade in such cases involves an attempt to *create* solutions that society lacks, such as a class for multiply handicapped children at a school where none exists. Such crusades often grow out of interaction in parents' associations, where mutual problems are discussed and shared definitions emerge.

Although parental entrepreneurship was the major mode of adjustment among the parents in my sample, I do not wish to suggest that all parents of severely handicapped children follow such a career path. My concern is only with showing *how* such a path can be established and implemented in a not entirely hospitable society. My major focus in this study, then, is on parental entrepreneurship as a social *role* based on a *definition of the situation* that may be seen as deviant by the larger society. My goal in the following chapters will be to explore the social processes through which this definition and role develop and to consider the implications of these processes for medical ethics and social change.

The ensuing chapters will be divided as follows: Chapter 1 will consist of a definitional and theoretical orientation and a review of the literature on stigma, self-esteem, and parental acceptance; Chapter 2 will continue the literature review in the area of parental careers and the professional-client relationship; Chapter 3 will include a summary of the research goals and expected findings of the study, as well as a discussion of the methods employed in the research; Chapters 4 and 5 will present the general tendencies of the parent data along with some cases in detail; Chapter 6 will present the pediatrician data; Chapter 7 will consist of a discussion of the findings of the study, especially in terms of the development of the role of parental entrepreneur; and Chapter 8 will deal with the conclusions and implications of the research.

NOTES

1. My use of the term, entrepreneurship, is suggested by Becker (1963) in his discussion of "moral entrepreneurs." In borrowing his use of the term, I wish to convey the idea of a similarly agressive form of enterprise designed to bring about change.

Chapter 1

QUALITY OF LIFE:
STIGMA AND THE DETERMINANTS
OF SELF-ESTEEM

Defining Quality of Life

This study began with the goal of evaluating the quality of life of physically and mentally handicapped children. Such quality of life has been linked in some cases with the *right* to life, and doctors have sometimes advocated withholding life-saving treatment from infants whose prognosis for "normal social adjustment" was low (see, for example, Lorber, 1971; Duff and Campbell, 1973). Typically, such prognosis is based on medical evaluation, on the assumption that social adjustment has a physiological basis.

Sociologists have shown, however, that social and cultural conditions are important determinants of the role that physical conditions play in shaping human behavior. The literature in medical sociology contains many examples of individuals with similar symptoms who recover at different rates as a result of such social variables as marital stability, ethnicity, and self-esteem. In order, then, to evaluate the eventual quality of life of a child born with a serious disability, one ought to take the child's social situation into account.

To determine the relevant social variables in such cases, one must first establish a measure of quality of life, a concept that is likely to depend on cultural values. A life of quality in one culture may be seen as valueless in aother. (Eaton and Weil [reported in Freidson, 1970] have shown, for example, that among the Hutterites, the "mentally ill" are given meaningful roles to perform.) Perhaps the least culture-bound definition of quality of life would be "the ability to adjust to the norms of a culture, regardless of the content of those norms." Such a definition still does not account for differential subcultural or individualistic adaptations. "Adjustment" to the norms of a majority culture is not necessarily "right" or "good," and many of the "great" people in history have not been "well-adjusted."

Another way of conceptualizing quality of life might be in terms of the perspective of the individual rather than that of society or the sociologist. Thus, if people are satisfied with their lives, those lives would be judged to be of quality, regardless of the views of others in society. Such a stance is related to pragmatist and existentialist philosophies and suggests that a subjective view that has meaning in everyday life may have greater validity than some absolute, objective standard. Seeing reality through the eyes of the person or group being studied is also related to the position taken by the so-called Chicago School of symbolic interaction theory.

The sociological concept that best describes a subjective view of quality of life is the *self*, particularly in its evaluative dimension. The self-concept is a heuristic one because sociologists have developed various means for discovering people's feelings about themselves. One might still argue that people who view their own lives as valuable might not be judged as socially worthy by others. The resolution of this issue may involve ethics rather than sociology. Yet, from a humanistic point of view, one ought at least to take into account the feelings of the individual in question in making such judgments of worth. This position guides the inquiry undertaken in the following study.

The Concept of Self-Esteem

The self-concept has been the subject of considerable attention in the area of symbolic interactionism. Its importance was noted early by such theorists as Mead, Cooley, and James, who suggested the interactional nature of people's knowledge and feelings about themselves. Mead has suggested that the self is acquired through role-taking, or the process of learning to understand the responses of other people to oneself. This conception of self has received empirical support in a number of studies. (see, for example, Miyamoto and Dornbusch, 1956; Quarantelli and Cooper, 1966; Videbeck, 1960).

Various measures of the self-concept, such as the Kuhn-McPartland Twenty Statements Test (Kuhn and McPartland, 1954) have revealed two major components of self: consensual and subconsensual. The consensual or cognitive side of the self-concept consists of knowledge about the self that is noncontroversial. In addition, the self also has a subconsensual component that is evaluative or affective. This attitudinal component of the self-concept has been called *self-esteem*.

Various studies have shown that high self-esteem, or having a positive attitude toward or acceptance of oneself, may be valuable as an index of adjustment. High self-esteem among children and adolescents, for example, has been shown to be correlated with better school performance, fewer psychosomatic symptoms, less anxiety and more participation in a variety of activities outside the home (Coopersmith, 1967; Rosenberg, 1965). Experimental studies have shown that people with high self-esteem have a greater willingness to perform (Jones, 1968).

Self-esteem, of course, is relative to one's normative reference point. As James (1890) has suggested:

$$\text{Self-esteem} = \frac{\text{Success}}{\text{Pretensions.}}$$

Hence, a number of studies have measured self-esteem and adjustment by comparing real self-concept with the ideal, that is, the kind of person one would like to be.

In studying the self-esteem of the handicapped, then, one should determine levels of aspiration, or the normative context of self-definition. If, in general, handicapped people judge themselves in terms of the standards society sets for normals, they are likely to have problems of adjustment. If, on the other hand, they are able to substitute idiosyncratic or subcultural criteria of success, they may very easily view themselves in a favorable light. The normative basis for the self-judgments of handicapped people is an empirical question.

The Labeling Perspective: The Effect of Societal Stigma

A number of writers have suggested that handicapped people are judged on the same basis as normals in society, resulting in a degradation or *stigmatization* of the handicapped. Studies of stigmatization have been closely allied with the "labeling perspective" in the sociology of deviance. Labeling theorists such as Becker (1963) and Lemert (1951) have argued that deviance is not an inherent condition of a person or act, but rather, refers to the imposition of a definition or label on people by a particular group of others who do not approve of their attributes or behavior. In American society, various groups of people have been labeled as deviant at one time or another: juvenile delinquents, racial minorities, homosexuals, drug addicts, the physically and mentally handicapped, among others.

Stigmatization, then, is a form of societal reaction to those members who are "different" and do not conform to an arbitrary set of expectations. As defined by Lemert (1967: 42), "stigmatization describes a process of attaching visible signs of moral inferiority to persons, such as invidious labels, marks, brands, or publicly disseminated information." In his analysis of the consequences of stigma for face-to-face interaction, Goffman (1963: 2-3) explains:

> While the stranger is present before us, evidence can arise of his possessing an attribute that makes him different from others in the category of persons available for him to be, and of a less desirable kind — in the extreme, a person who is quite thoroughly bad, or dangerous, or weak. He is thus reduced in our minds from a whole and usual person to a tainted, discounted one. Such an attribute is a stigma, especially when its discrediting effect is very extensive; sometimes it is also called a failing, a shortcoming, a handicap. It constitutes a special discrepancy between virtual and actual social identity.

As Hewett (1970: 204) has noted, society is actually ambiguous in its attitudes toward and expectations for the handicapped. The handicapped are expected to "adjust" to and "accept" their handicaps and at the same time to "deny" them by acting as "normal" as possible. The handicapped are expected to work, but the physical accommodations at most jobs are not suitable. The mother is told to treat her handicapped child "as a normal child," but the child is denied access to normal schools and other facilities. The disabled are thus stigmatized because they are not normal but, at the same time, they are denied the opportunities to *be* normal by the society that stigmatizes them. A similar situation also exists in the case of other stigmatized groups, such as ex-convicts who are not given jobs or ex-mental patients who are never again completely trusted by their families. As Scheff (1966), Lemert (1967), Becker (1963), Ray (1964), and others have shown, such continued labeling can become a self-fulfilling prophecy. The stigmatized are thrust back into their deviant roles, because no other roles are open to them. (Then, of course, the cycle repeats itself when the "deviants" are criticized by society for their deviance.)

One of the main consequence of being stigmatized by society is the acceptance of a deviant self-image, an outcome consistent with "looking-glass self" theory. Thus, labeled individuals see themselves as society sees them, as morally inferior people (Lemert, 1967; Goffman, 1963). According to Goffman (1963: 32ff.), such self-derogation has a variable onset, even in the case of the congenitally handicapped. While some children with an inborn stigma learn of their disadvantageous position at an early age, others may be shielded by their families from negative definitions. Eventually, however, the child will be exposed to the evaluations of the larger society, and a "moral experience" will occur. Goffman notes that school entrance is often the first occasion of stigma learning both for those in regular and in special schools.[1] Of those who are sent to special schools for the handicapped, Goffman (1963: 33) writes, "(The child) will be told that he will have an easier time of it among 'his own,' and thus learns that the own he thought he possessed was the wrong one, and that this lesser own is really his." If children somehow manage to survive the early school years without becoming fully aware of their stigma, Goffman suggests that they will face "the moment of truth" with the beginning of dating or employment-seeking in the teen years.

Other studies have noted a phenomenon that might be called "stigma transference": through a process of "guilt by association," family members and others who are close to a stigmatized individual come to share some of the stigma (Goffman calls theirs' a "courtesy stigma"). Studies of wives of mental patients and ex-mental patients (Freeman and Simmons, 1961; Schwartz, 1956), for example, show a great concern about a derogatory evaluation of the family by the community. As a result, the wives would often attempt to define the situation in more socially acceptable terms, such as those of physical illness. In general, "the closer the definer is socially and emotionally to the person whose behavior is under consideration, the greater will be the tendency to utilize the normality framework in interpreting the behavior" (Schwartz, 1957: 297).

The use of a "normality framework" is also characteristic of face-to-face interaction between the stigmatized person and normals. In the case of a *discreditable* stigma (Goffman, 1963), that is, one that is not readily apparent (such as having a prison record or a disfigurement hidden by clothing), the stigmatized often try to deny their stigma and "pass" as normal.[2] Visible handicaps such as those to be included in this study, on the other hand, fall within Goffman's *discredited* category — they pose an immediate threat to nonproblematic interaction between the stigmatized and the normal. Davis (1961) suggests that interaction between the visibly handicapped and the normal proceeds through three stages of "normalization." At first, normals engages in "fictional acceptance" of the handicapped, pretending not to notice their stigmatizing features. This stage is ideally followed by "breaking through" in which reciprocal role-taking around a normalized projection of self occurs. In breaking through, normals accept the handicapped as their moral equals. Finally, after a time, the stigmatized's moral normality becomes institutionalized with only situational qualifications. This sequence of stages is more the exception than the rule, however, and often normals never accept the handicapped in more than a fictionalized manner. These observations are supported in an experimental study by Kleck et al. (1966).

One way in which the stigmatized cope with the difficulties of interaction with normals is through subculture formation (Lemert, 1967; Becker, 1963). Goffman (1963) suggests that stigmatized people feel most comfortable in interaction with two groups: the "own" and the "wise." The own are those who share the same stigma. With them, the stigmatized can relax, knowing the group recognizes them as multifaceted human beings rather than merely the bearers of a stigmatizing attribute. Other members of the stigmatized person's "in-group" are the wise, normals who have broken through, in Davis' terminology. A person can become wise in a variety of ways, probably the most common of which is to be a member of the stigmatized's family. Other wise people are those whose employment brings them into contact with the stigmatized: nurses, physical therapists, probation officers. Goffman suggests that few normals become wise by choice, because the wise share a courtesy stigma with their associates.

All of the literature on stigma, then, depicts the stigmatized as targets of society's moral indignation. They are labeled as inferior by others, and as a result negatively label themselves as well. Consequently, their self-esteem is low, and they are likely to have problems of adjustment. One might expect, then, that many children and adults born with severe birth defects would be more or less maladjusted.

Studies of Self-Esteem in the Handicapped: The Myth of Maladjustment

Psychoanalytic theory has classically posited a strong relationship between people's feelings about their bodies and their level of psychological adjustment. As a result, psychoanalytically oriented psychiatrists and psychologists tend to be somewhat suspicious of the mental well-being of persons with bodily aberrations of various kinds. Bernabeu (1958) argues that the young polio patients in her study used inappropriate and pathogenic defenses to handle feelings of frustration, anxiety, and rage, and in an evaluation of orthopedically handicapped children, Schechter (1961) notes an "ever-present thinly disguised depression in all these children." Such studies have been done in the hospital, and hospitalized children might be expected to show some depression simply because they are away from home and subject to the pain and discomfort of various medical and surgical procedures, *apart from* any handicap they might possess.

Another type of psychoanalytically based study has employed projective techniques to evaluate the self-esteem and emotional problems of children with handicaps. A popular technique in studies of this type has been the Draw-A-Person test, in which subjects are asked to draw a person of each sex and then to draw themselves. The DAP, like other projective techniques, has been criticized for its questionable validity, reliability, and meaning. (For example, see Wylie, 1974: 260-265). Using the technique, Wysocki and Whitney (1965) found, in a comparison of 50 crippled and 50 noncrippled children, that the crippled children showed greater feelings of inferiority (large size figures' being interpreted as a form of negative compensation), anxiety, and aggression ("evidenced" through pressure and shading).

In other studies using the DAP, trained judges were *unable to distinguish* the figure drawings of handicapped children from those of a nonhandicapped control group. In an analysis of the drawings of 22 polio cases, Silverstein and Robinson (1956) found that judges who knew *in advance* that their subjects were disabled found evidence of these disabilities in their drawings. In a second stage of the study, a normal matched control group was added, and the judges were no longer able to tell the drawings of the two groups apart. Similarly, in a study of 26 children with upper extremity amputation and a matched control group (Centers and Centers, 1963), judges were able to distinguish *self*-portraits of amputees from those of the nonamputees but could *not* distinguish the general Draw-A-Person. Further, the amputee children did not show greater conflict or anxiety. The authors concluded (Centers and Centers, 1963: 165), "the general conclusion from the investigation is that amputee children in the Draw-A-Person Test in the main represent their bodies and those of others realistically and, on the whole, nondefensively."

All of these figure-drawing studies have used "body image" as an index of self-concept on the assumption that the two are highly correlated. Such a correlation should be empirically demonstrated. Secord and Jourard (1953) found a moderate correlation between attitudes toward body and self. Rosen and Ross (1968) have noted a similar finding and have shown further the role played by the intervening variable of importance: subjects' satisfaction with the parts of their bodies was correlated with their self-concepts *when such body satisfaction was important to them*. Perhaps then, handicapped children could have high self-esteem if they were socialized into believing that physical prowess was not an important consideration in evaluating people. This possibility is supported by a study (Dow, 1966) in which parents of handicapped children generally depreciated the importance of physique and were thus able to maintain optimistic attitudes toward their children's disabilities.

Thus, studies using the variable of body image have not demonstrated any clear-cut feelings of inferiority among the disabled. The labeling theorists' contention that stigmatized individuals accept society's definition of them is consequently open to question. Some support for the labeling position can be found in a few studies that measured self-esteem in other ways. For example, using a "self-derogation index" designed for young children, Meyerowitz (1962) found that a group of educable mentally retarded youngsters attending a regular school had more negative self-concepts than a normal group. Similarly, when presented with a series of pictures of handicapped and nonhandicapped children, *both* the nonhandicapped *and* the handicapped children in one study (Richardson et al., 1961) chose the picture of a nonhandicapped child as the one they liked best. (The subjects in this study were not *severely* handicapped, however, and a small number of severely handicapped children who were tested showed different results.) Perhaps those with the least severe handicaps, who are consequently the most closely integrated in normal society, are more likely to be exposed to and to accept stigmatizing definitions of themselves.[3]

In another study (Richardson et al., 1964), children with slight-to-moderate physical handicaps were asked to talk about themselves. The handicapped children made a slightly larger proportion of negative statements about themselves than the nonhandicapped group (13% versus 8% for boys; 17% versus 11% for girls). As the authors' percentages indicate (although the authors do not themselves suggest such an interpretation), from 83% to 87% of the statements the handicapped children made about themselves were *positive*. The authors did note that the self-descriptions given by the handicapped were realistic, a finding noted also by Meyerowitz in the study cited above.

Other studies that have measured self-concept directly have not supported the contention that stigmatized individuals accept society's definition of them. In a comparison of 29 congenitally blind with an equal number of sighted children, for example, Zunich and Ledwith (1965) found little difference in self-esteem between the two groups. Similarly, Mayer (1967) found that retarded children do not necessarily have low self-esteem, and Shelsky (1957) found no difference in the self-concept of adult amputees and normal controls. Collins et al. (1970) found significant differences between retarded and nonretarded adolescents in some aspects of self-concept but not others. Generally, self-esteem was low in *both* groups. Finally, Krider (1959) found that crippled children attending a special school did not have significantly different self-concepts from a matched control group of normal children.

Another group of studies has considered the variable of *degree* of disability as a factor in self-esteem. Smits (1964) found, for example, that severely disabled adolescents attending normal schools had significantly lower self-concept scores than adolescents with mild disabilities. In addition, severely disabled females had significantly lower scores than severely disabled males. Another study (Meissner et al., 1967), using a sample of high school juniors, found *no* correlation between obviousness or impact of disability and self-concept. When sex was held constant, however, females with the highest impact and most obvious disabilties had negative self-concepts, while similarly disabled males had high self-esteem. This latter finding concurs with the sex difference found by Smits. In another study (Goldy and Katz, 1971), the degree to which children with hemophilia felt "different" was not correlated with the number and severity of illness episodes, but rather, the degree to which they were isolated from normal activities. Finally, in a sociometric study of 10 to 14 years olds in a day school for the handicapped (Cruickshank and Medve, 1948), those with the greatest degree of disability were the least accepted by their classmates. However, the degree of *obviousness* of their disabilities had no relationship to acceptance. This study did not measure self-concept directly.[4] Thus, degree of disability seems to have some relationship with self- and other-acceptance, but the relationship is not consistent or clear-cut.

In summary, then, studies of the self-esteem of handicapped children and adults do *not* unconditionally support the suggestion of the labeling theorists that social stigma produces lack of self-acceptance and consequent maladjustment. An important question raised by these finding is: what determines various levels of self-esteem and adjustment in handicapped children? and conjointly: by what processes do some of these children overcome the effects of societal stigma while others succumb to its pressure?

The Concept of Reference Group as an Explanation of Varying Levels of Adjustment

In the case of another stigmatized group, Black people, sociologists and psychologists argued for a long time that the group's minority racial status would produce low self-esteem in comparison with whites. Recent studies, however, have cast considerable doubt on this argument. In fact, almost all of the recent literature suggests that Blacks, including children, have self-esteem as high or higher than corresponding groups of whites. In attempting to explain this apparently incongruent phenomenon, Rosenberg and Simmons (1971) have noted that Black children in predominantly Black schools have higher self-esteem than those in schools where they are in the minority. They suggest that children interact primarily in primary groups of others like themselves and that these groups serve to insulate them from societal definitions and protect their self-esteem. The interpretation of Rosenberg and Simmons corresponds entirely with symbolic interactionist theory of "universes of discourse," "reference groups," and "significant others."

Thus, in order to understand the self-conceptions of handicapped children, one must ascertain the definitions they receive from various members of their reference sets. The literature suggests that handicapped children will have positive self-concepts if they are defined positively by their significant others and negative self-concepts if their significant others do not evaluate them highly. Identifying the significant persons and groups who constitute the reference set of the handicapped child thus becomes important.

Richardson (1969) argues that, unlike members of racial minorities, the handicapped are not surrounded by others like themselves. On the contrary, he asserts, those around the handicapped person are likely to share the negative cultural definition. His assertion seems to rest on his picture selection studies and studies suggesting that normals typically do not initiate contacts with the handicapped. He does *not* show, however, that these normals are the major reference group of the handicapped. The literature in fact suggests that the handicapped are likely to be isolated from interaction with normals. (Richardson himself speaks about the "impoverished social environment" of handicapped children.) Significant relationships are unlikely to develop in the absence of interactional opportunities. One might expect, then, that the self-concepts of the severely handicapped would be formed through interaction with what Goffman calls the own and the wise.

The Reference Groups of Handicapped Children: The Importance of Parents as Significant Others

All of the literature in the field of child development suggests that until adolescence, and possibly afterward as well, children's most important significant others are their parents. The importance of parents as the primary socializing agents for their children makes sense theoretically and has been demonstrated empirically in numerous studies. High parent-child correlations have been found on attitudes ranging from religion and politics to self and role.

Various studies have clarified the processes through which parental definitions are translated into children's self-definitions. For example, Rosenberg (1965) and Coopersmith (1967) have shown that the interactional contexts within which parental definitions are issued may affect children's perceptions of those definitions. Diagram 1 illustrates some of the variables involved in the transmission of definitions that determine children's self-esteem.

For the purposes of the present study, one must inquire whether the significant others of handicapped children are the same as those of normal children. One would expect that for handicapped children living at home, the parents would be just as important as or more important than the parents of nonhandicapped children. Because children with severe handicaps tend to be somewhat more sheltered than other children, their most frequent and intense interactions are even more likely than those of normal children to be with parents and other family members. This expectation is supported by Richardson et al. (1964), who report that the handicapped children they interviewed showed less interpersonal experience outside the family than a comparable nonhandicapped group.

The role of parents in the adjustment of severely handicapped children is strongly suggested by one psychiatric and social evaluation of 13 cases of children with myelomeningocele:

All of the children with a poor adaptation were offspring of parents with poor adaptation. Parents with good-to-fair adaptation produced children with a comparable level of adjustment in all but one instance. Three children of parents with poor adaptation were able to achieve a higher adjustment level; in these cases the acceptance and support given by older siblings was a vital factor in their development [Kolin, 1971: 1017-1018].

The study found further that the effect of parental adaptation was the crucial determining variable regardless of the level of physical impairment of the child.

A number of other studies have also demonstrated a correlation between parental attitudes and behavior and the adjustment of handicapped children (Heilman, 1950; Grebler, 1952). In one study (Denhoff and Holden, 1954, 1971), children with cerebral palsy who made the best school adjustment had the most "accepting" parents. However, part of the measure of parental acceptance used in the study was trust in the judgments of professional personnel and initiative

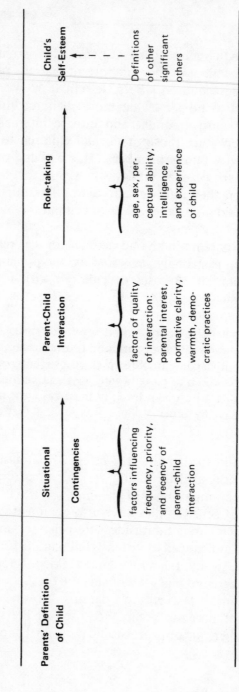

Parents' Definition of Child

Situational Contingencies	Parent-Child Interaction	Role-taking	Child's Self-Esteem
factors influencing frequency, priority, and recency of parent-child interaction	factors of quality of interaction: parental interest, normative clarity, warmth, democratic practices	age, sex, perceptual ability, intelligence, and experience of child	Definitions of other significant others

DIAGRAM 1: The Determinants of a Child's Self-Esteem

to "carry out professional recommendations." Thus, "non-accepting" parents were described as being highly critical of school and medical personnel. Undoubtedly, parents who define the school situation in negative terms are likely to have children with similar definitions, resulting in "poor school adjustment." Such a definition is likely to prevail *regardless* of how good or nurturant or accepting these parents are toward their children. The crucial variable, then, might be parents' acceptance of *school* rather than of their child. Perhaps the investigators in the study were operating under a professional bias, resulting in a negative attitude toward parents who do not follow professional advice. This kind of bias will be discussed more fully in later chapters. In any case, Denhoff and Holden *have* demonstrated a strong correlation between parental attitudes and the performance of their handicapped children.

While *parents* are almost certainly the most important members of the handicapped child's reference set, other persons and groups also must be included: siblings, extended family members, neighbors, physicians and other medical professionals, teachers, clergymen, other handicapped and nonhandicapped children and adults. While all of these people no doubt play a role in the socialization of the handicapped child, the literature suggests that *parents* remain the major, most significant definers of self- and adjustment-related attitudes that these children encounter. Thus, parents become the focus of the following study.

NOTES

1. Richardson (1970) notes that after the age of six, children's attitudes toward physical handicaps are as negative as those of their parents. Goodman et al. (1963) have demonstrated, however, that some cultural variability exists, and Jewish

children are less likely than others to concur in majority attitudes toward physical disability.

2. Some of the strains inherent in "passing" are discussed in Messinger (1962).

3. In a sociometric study of a summer camp for both handicapped and nonhandicapped children (Richardson, 1971), however, the handicapped were likely to choose other handicapped children rather than normals. Thus, while the handicapped might select a picture of a nonhandicapped person in an experimental study, in real, everyday, social relationships, they do not favor the normal group over their own. The choice of a peer over a sociometric "star" in the context of informal social relationships has also been reported elsewhere in all normal samples (Thibaut, 1950; Jennings, 1950).

4. Mayer (1967) has shown in fact that self-concept is not necessarily correlated with sociometric status.

Chapter 2

VICTIM-BLAMING AND
PARENTAL ACCEPTANCE

The Sources of Parental Definitions of their Children:
Antecedent Conditions

If parents are the most important significant others for
handicapped children, the evaluation such children receive
from their parents should be a crucial determinant of their
self-esteem. An important question, then, is: What causes
parents to evaluate their children in a positive or negative
fashion? While the relationship between parental evaluation
of children and children's self-evaluations has received considerable attention in the literature, a lesser amount of
research has been devoted to the question just raised. An important focus of the present research, then, is the process
through which parents arrive at differential definitions of
their children.

The literature contains a number of studies, generally
undertaken from a psychoanalytic point of view, that seem to
assume at the outset that parents are likely to reject their
handicapped children. When the findings are contrary to this
assumption, they are typically explained as evidence of denial

on the part of parents who are attempting to assuage their guilt. Thus, even parents who claim to accept their handicaped children are defined as hiding their real feelings of rejection. If this interpretation were correct, handicapped children would be expected to have universally negative self-concepts as a result of parental rejection. As indicated earlier, however, self-esteem among the handicapped seems to be as variable as it is among the normal. Thus, any blanket assumption about *all* the parents of the handicapped is unsupported. Most studies define parental acceptance/rejection as a *variable* dependent on a variety of antecedent parental traits and/or continuing situational factors. This study will be based on such a definition.

The theoretical position that will be taken is that definitions of people and events are constantly changing interactional products, a basic tenet of Meadian symbolic interactionism. This study will be concerned, then, with the process development of parents' definitions of their children and of the situations they face in everyday life. In its consideration of process, the study should help to explain the role of timing in definitional formation and change, including an evaluation of the relative importance of priority versus recency.

In order to evaluate the role of time in the development of parents' definitions, four periods that correspond to or include major turning points will be emphasized: (1) prenatal — parents' socialization prior to the birth of their handicapped child, (2) birth — initial reactions to the birth of the child, or, in some cases, of the delayed knowledge that "something is wrong" with the baby, (3) postpartum and later infancy — the factors involved in accepting the reality of the birth of a chronically disabled child, as well as the continuing adjustment of the family once the child's problem is diagnosed and the child is living at home and interacting in society, and (4) childhood — the effects of more recent interactional developments.

THE PRENATAL PERIOD:
PARENTS' PRIOR SOCIALIZATION

Earlier studies have emphasized the role of preexisting parental traits in determing parents' reactions to their children. Some psychologists (Shirley, 1941; Behrens, 1954) have stressed the importance of the mother's personality in her approach to her children. Anthropologists and sociologists, on the other hand, have suggested cultural and subcultural determinants of parental attitudes toward their children, emphasizing such factors as social class, race, ethnicity, and religion (see, for example, Havighurst and Davis, 1955; Kohn, 1959, 1963; Rainwater, 1966; Elkin, 1960; Stycos, 1955).

In the case of parents of congenitally handicapped children, various preexisting parental traits have been cited as important in determining parental acceptance and rejection. Psychoanalytically oriented studies tend to focus on personality defects with a basis in a parent's own childhood. In one study of a handicap with later onset — poliomyelitis (Westlund and Palumbo, 1946), parental rejection was found to depend on the parent-child relationship that had existed when the child was healthy, especially where the child's handicap interfered with some selfish parental need.

A number of studies have looked at the relationship between social class and parental acceptance of handicapped children. Dow (1966) found no correlation between social class and acceptance and noted that parents of all classes tended to have optimistic attitudes toward their children's physical disabilities. In the case of mental handicaps, different results have been reported. One study (Downey, 1963) found that more educated families tended to show less interest in their institutionalized children, because such children were unable to conform to the family's career expectations. Similar findings have been reported by Holt (1958).

In an insightful article, Mercer (1965) suggests that the very definition of a person as "mentally retarded" is rooted in professional, middle-class values. In a study of institutionalized retarded chldren who were either discharged to their families or remained in the institution, she found that those who were discharged generally came from low-status families. High-status families generally concurred with official definitions of retardation and were not optimistic about their children's futures. The low-status families, on the other hand, could envision their children's playing normal adult roles. Thus, while social class may be unrelated to parental acceptance in the case of physical handicaps, lower-class parents seem to be more accepting of children with mental handicaps than their middle- and upper-class counterparts.

Another background factor that has been explored in connection with parental acceptance is religion. Leichman (reported in Jordan, 1962) found Protestant and Catholic mothers to be equally accepting of their retarded children. Zuk (1959a), however, has reported that Catholic mothers in one sample were more acceptant of their retarded children than Protestants and Jews. He argues that Catholics are absolved from guilt by their religious beliefs, and that Catholic doctrine insists that every child, normal or defective, is a special gift of God. Yet, in another study (Boles, 1959), Catholic mothers were found to have *more* feelings of guilt than Protestants and Jews. Zuk's finding might be explained in another way, however. As Durkheim classically postulated, Catholic society tends to be more closely integrated than that of other religions. Its members are therefore more likely to receive social support than members of other societies. Perhaps then, social support, and not religion, is the important variable. Indeed, Wortis and Margolies (1955) have reported that the parents of cerebral palsied children in their sample who made the best adjustment were those with interested friends and relatives.

Jews tend to have a closely knit society. However, unlike the Catholic case, Jewish groups are not always supportive in this situation. Saenger (reported in Zuk, 1962) has noted a higher percentage of institutionalization of mental defectives among Jews than Italians. Jewish cultural values tend to stress education and achievement, ideals that are incompatible with retardation. Thus, acceptance may be related to close integration in a *supportive* social network.

In another study (Zuk et al., 1961), mothers rating themselves as intense in their religious practices were judged to be slightly more acceptant of their retarded children. Kolin (1971) had a similar finding in a very small sample of families of children with myelomeningocele. Again, however, strength of religious belief may simply indicate immersion in a closely knit social network.

Another variable that seems to be correlated with parental acceptance is the age of the child. Wortis and Margolies (1955) and Zuk (1959a) have reported greater acceptance by parents of *younger* handicapped children. As Wortis and Margolies suggest, problems of social acceptance are likely to increase with the age of the child, and Birenbaum (1971) has noted that maintaining a "normal-appearing round of life" becomes more difficult as a retarded child gets older. However, Meyerowitz and Kaplan (1967) suggest that in the case of cystic fibrosis, family stress reactions are greater when the child is younger. The nature of the disease might be important here. Diagnosis of a condition that is likely to be fatal in addition to chronically disabling might have greater impact at first than a condition whose disabling and stigmatizing nature becomes more apparent as a child grows older.

Another trait that might play a role in parental acceptance is a parent's *self*-acceptance. Medinnus and Curtis (1963), for example, have shown a high correlation between maternal self-acceptance and mothers' acceptance of their children. They do not show, however, whether self-acceptance *prior to* childbirth is correlated with later child-acceptance. Parental self-acceptance might in fact be *contingent upon* child-acceptance ("I must be a good parent because I produced a good child"). One study of mothers of retarded children (Cummings, 1966) did reveal a lower "sense of maternal competence" than that found in a control group. However, the mothers of the retarded did *not* have lower levels of general self-esteem.

Another area of parental socialization that might have a bearing on parents' acceptance of their children is their prior experience with children in general, and handicapped children in particular. In their study of parents of myelomeningocele children, for example, Kolin (1971) found that those parents who made the best adjustment were those who had a normal child prior to the birth of the defective one. The presence of other siblings is an advantage also noted by Wortis and Margolies (1955). On the other hand, Meyerowitz and Kaplan (1967) found greater stress in families that had two or more children with cystic fibrosis. Thus, the health status of siblings seems to be important.

Other factors that seem to be correlated with parental acceptance in some cases are length and stability of the marital relationship and whether the pregnancy in question was planned or unplanned (Kolin, 1971). Another factor that might be related to adjustment is the age of the parents. Older, more experienced, parents might be able to adapt better. However, younger parents might have an advantage in still having the opportunity to bear other (normal) children.

All of these background variables, in turn, would be expected to give rise to parents' definitions values, norms, and expectations regarding children and handicapped children. Do parents define children as an important and necessary part of marriage or do they see them as incidental to marital happiness? Do they expect their children to have certain qualities, such as a particular sex, physical attractiveness, intelligence or athletic ability, or to play a specific role in family life? Coopersmith (1967) found a correlation between child's self-esteem and mother's reason for having children. Of the children with high self-esteem, 67.6% of the mothers saw having children as a natural event, while 32.4% wanted children for personal reasons. Perhaps mothers who see children as a natural event do not push their children into meeting unrealistic goals and are more satisfied with their child's performance at any level. As Wortis and Margolies (1955: 114) noted about families that had made a successful adjustment to their child's cerebral palsy, "There were no great expectations for the child, and there was shared pleasure in caring for him." Thus, parents' conceptions of the ideal child might have a bearing on their satisfaction with their real child.

The relationship between parental conceptions of their real and ideal child was explored by Worchel and Worchel (1961). They found a larger discrepancy between real and ideal when parents rated their retarded chldren than when they rated their children's normal siblings. However, parents did not rate their retarded children significantly less favorably than they rated "most other (normal) children." The investigators also found great variability in parental attitudes toward their retarded children, suggesting again the implausibility of the psychoanalytically based contention that parents unanimously reject their handicapped offspring.

A major contention of this study is that preexsting parental traits and attitudes (with the exception of such fixed characteristics as race or having had a child previously) are likely to change in the course of social interaction. Even parents who have definite preexisting prejudices about handicapped children might eventually be accepting of their handicapped child as a result of situational and interactional contingencies following the birth of the child. This possibility is illustrated by a case cited by Hare (1966: 758):

Case 8 — Spina bifida cystica.
Parents aged 17; first child. Mother had been told the baby was never likely to walk. At the first interview she said she would much rather the baby died, as if the child were a cripple

she wouldn't know how to look after her. Father intervened with, "She doesn't love the baby yet as she should; she hasn't handled her much, but she'll come to it." At the six-month interview the mother was reported to be "terribly fond of her baby."

Thus, once a child is born, its parents continue to interact with both old and new significant others, and with one new significant other in particular — the child. (See Bell, 1968 for a convincing argument for the often overlooked influence of the *child* as a socializing agent for the *parents*.) A basic expectation of this study, then, is:

> Parental definitions will be a function of an interaction between preexisting orientations and interactional experience following the birth of the child.

The entire process, in which parents' definition of their child and child's self-esteem are key variables, is represented in Diagram 2.

Thus, parents' definition of their child at any given time is expected to derive from: (1) preexisting and changing orientations toward children and toward handicaps, (2) parents' self-esteem, (3) child's self-esteem and performance, (4) evaluations of the child by parents' significant others, and (5) parent-child interaction. The relative effect of each of these elements is, in turn, expected to be contingent on:

(a) parents' role-taking ability.

(b) frequency, duration, and intensity of interaction. As Kinch (1968) and others have suggested, definitions heard most often and over the longest period of time, as well as those issued most forcefully, are likely to have the greatest influence. Various situational contingencies are likely to play a role in frequency, duration, and intensity (see section d below).

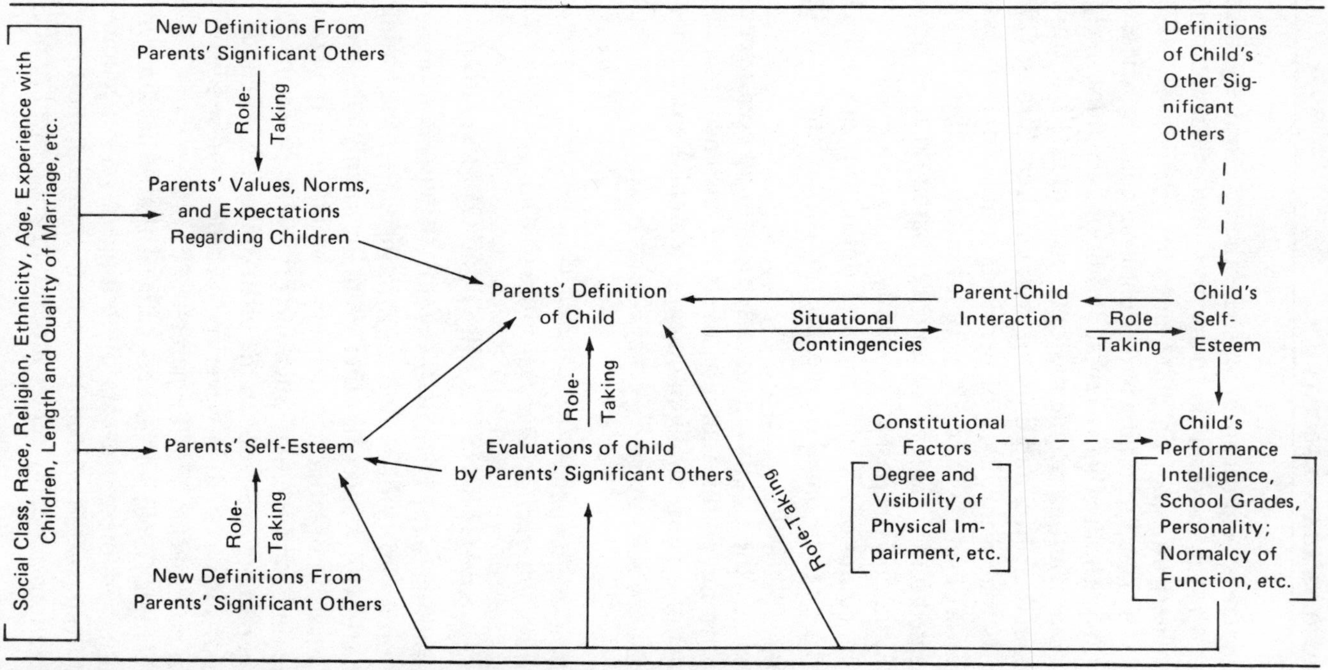

Parents' Prior Socialization

Social Class, Race, Religion, Ethnicity, Age, Experience with Children, Length and Quality of Marriage, etc.

New Definitions From Parents' Significant Others

Role-Taking

Parents' Values, Norms, and Expectations Regarding Children

Parents' Definition of Child

Role-Taking

Evaluations of Child by Parents' Significant Others

Role-Taking

Parents' Self-Esteem

Role-Taking

New Definitions From Parents' Significant Others

Situational Contingencies

Constitutional Factors

Degree and Visibility of Physical Impairment, etc.

Parent-Child Interaction

Role-Taking

Child's Self-Esteem

Definitions of Child's Other Significant Others

Child's Performance

Intelligence, School Grades, Personality; Normalcy of Function, etc.

DIAGRAM 2: Sources of Parents' Definitions of Children and Children's Self-Esteem

(c) relative significance of the other. Those significant others who are most salient to an individual are likely to have the greatest influence on mind and self.

(d) the effects of timing and situational contingencies. One might hypothesize that parental definitions are most likely to change at various accidental and institutionalized turning points in their lives and those of their children. Strauss (1962) suggests that recognition of personal continuity is necessary to a sense of self. As a result, people tend to see their lives as a connected and meaningful sequence, based on their present condition, and the past is constantly being redefined in terms of that condition. Thus, parental definitions are probably most likely to be based on the most *recent* turning point they have encountered.

Some of the significant others, situational contingencies, and turning points that are likely to be encountered by parents of a congenitally handicapped child are described in the following sections.

Career Development:
Postnatal Interaction and Definitional Change

BIRTH: REACTIONS TO FIRST INFORMATION

⌈Reactions to the birth of any child will depend, to some extent, on a variety of situational contingencies: the timing of the birth with respect to other events in family life, the ease and duration of labor and delivery, conditions at the hospital at the time, and the like. Such factors would no doubt play a role in parents' reactions to the birth of a defective child. The birth of such a child, however, poses a new and serious situational contingency for the parents.⌉

McHugh (1968) and others suggest that a person's interpretation of present events in contingent on expectations derived from past experience. In the birth situation, most parents' expectations probably center around an anticipated nondefective child. Most parents also have preconceived notions about the usual sequence of events in the delivery room. Mothers of spina bifida children, for example, who are awake for the birth report having recognized immediately that the behavior of the delivery room personnel did not "fit" the "theme" of birth of a normal child. Mothers note such clues as "the look on the nurse's face," consultations between the midwives or nurses in hushed voices, remarks made by medical students and nurses, nurses who "looked at each other and pointed at something," or "who were huddled in one corner," and often, the immediate transfer of the baby to a special care nursery, sometimes without showing the child to the mother (Walker, 1971; D'Arcy, 1968). The situation is typically one of "suspicion awareness" as described by Glaser and Strauss (1964), as in the case of dying patients who are not told the truth about their condition.

"Revelation"[1] also occurs in a variety of ways, but the first explanation of the baby's condition seems to range from overoptimism to overpessimism. The British literature on myelomeningocele contains many references to midwives who minimize the seriousness of the baby's condition, with remarks such as: "There is a small piece of skin missing from his back," "He has a small lump on the spine," "Nothing that a skin graft won't help," or "Just a small pimple on her back. . . . Nothing to worry about." (Walker, 1971; D'Arcy, 1968).

Less than half of the parents of spina bifida babies in one study (Freeston, 1971) had heard of the condition before the birth of their child, and only a few felt that they fully understood the first explanation given to them by the nursing staff. Some were merely told that their child had spina bifida with no further explanation at all (D'Arcy, 1968), while at the other extreme, some received long, detailed explanations in technical terms they did not understand (D'Arcy, 1968; Walker, 1971). In a few instances, parents have been left to discover the defect for themselves (Hare, 1966). Similar situations have been reported by parents of infants with other defects. A group of parents of Down's Syndrome children (Horrobin and Rynders, n.d.) have written about doctors who told them not to get too attached to their children or exerted pressure on them or have their babies institutionalized. Many noted that they felt isolated in the hospital, where they were ignored by the staff and not given any information.

Parents' frustrations in obtaining information in this situation are typical of other situations of doctor-patient interaction as well. As Freidson (1970) has suggested, the framework within which hospital interactions occur is one of "professional dominance." The physician, according to Freidson, rationalizes this position in the following way:

> The argument...asserts that, lacking professional training, the client is too ignorant to be able to comprehend what information he gets and that he is, in any case, too upset at being ill to be able to use the information he does get in a manner that is rational and responsible. From this it follows that giving information to the patient does not help him, but rather upsets him and creates additional "management problems" for the physician...Characteristically, the professional does not view the client as an adult, responsible person [1970: 142].

Davis (1960) has shown, similarly, how in the case of poliomyelitis, parents are given an overoptimistic picture by medical personnel who are aware that the prognosis for their children is not good. He quotes a treatment-staff member who said, "We try not to tell them too much. It's better if they find out for themselves in a natural sort of way " (1960: 44). For most parents, the "natural way" amounted to a painfully slow process in which their expectations for a complete recovery dwindled away. The doctors rationalized their approach with the argument that the truth would not be understood by the parents and would only make them "unmanageable."

Glaser and Strauss (1964) have noted similar professional reactions in the case of the dying patient, and Quint (1965) found professionals to be evasive and overoptimistic in a study of mastectomy patients. The latter study also noted techniques employed by nurses to avoid interaction with patients concerning their fears about cancer: they would change the subject, try to look busy, focus on specific treatments rather than a patient's general condition, or refrain from obtaining information so they could honestly say, "I don't know."

In most cases, both parents and professionals describe the reaction to the initial information that a child is defective as one of shock, disbelief, grief, tension, loss, helplessness, confusion, disappointment, anger, sorrow, frustration, anxiety, or physical exhaustion (see Tisza, 1962; Eisenstadt, 1971; Salk, 1972; Zuk, 1962; Meadow, 1968; and Farber, 1960, among others). In addition, mothers report feelings of isolation as a result of being separated from other mothers on maternity wards, while fathers sometimes are too disturbed to immediately return to work (Walker, 1971).

Professionals in the field, especially those with a psychoanalytic orientation, commonly argue that parents are also beset by guilt when they learn that they have produced a defective child (see, for example, Tisza, 1962; Zuk, 1962; Reid, 1971; Baum, 1962; Waterman, 1948; Mandelbaum and Wheeler, 1960; Farber, 1960; Salk, 1972). Consequently, parents of retarded children have been said to use such defense mechanisms as denial (Baum, 1962; Reid, 1971; Kanner, 1953; McCollum and Gisbon, 1970; Miller, 1968; Solnit and Stark, 1961), searching for nonexistent causes or cures (Kanner, 1953; Mandelbaum and Wheeler, 1960), returning to work, having another child (Mandelbaum and Wheeler, 1960), withdrawal (Reid, 1971), projection in the form of blaming the abnormality on an early "accident," falsification of memory, or developing a "martyr complex" in which the deficiency is seen as "an act of God" (Waterman, 1948). Farber (1960) suggests that a "nervous condition" is likely to ensue if these defenses are not adequate. In support of this suggestion, he shows that in a sample of mothers with severely retarded children, those who had been treated for a nervous condition had greater initial impact after their child's diagnosis. The psychoanalytic argument is not supported emprically by any of the writers who present it.

[In some cases, birth defects are not recognized until sometime after a baby leaves the hospital. In such instances, parents must learn to redefine their children as "sick" after they have already defined them as "healthy." Particularly in the case of invisible defects, parents are likely to question medical opinion. As Jordan (1971) has noted, many parents are not aware of the normal timing of developmental milestones, and babies are *expected* to be dependent. Thus, parents might find it hard to believe that their children, who are late in holding objects alone or sitting up by themselves, are retarded or have cerebral palsy. Professionals sometimes attribute such disbelief to guilt and denial.]

Sometimes, parents are aware that something is wrong with their child *before* they are informed by a medical professional. Meyerowitz and Kaplan (1967) report greater stress among parents of children with cystic fibrosis when diagnosis was delayed, and Hewett (1970) reports that, in a study of parents of children with cerebral palsy, 90% of the mothers thought that something was wrong with their babies before they were diangosed. When doctors did not immediately concur with their assessment, anxiety increased. One of the mothers in her study described the experience as follows:

Well, I told them at the clinic and they wouldn't believe me. When he was about 4 or 5 months old — give him a rattle or anything like that, a baby will hold it and *he* wouldn't, he just — put it into his hand, his hand would just open and he'd drop it. And they just called me stupid, at the clinic. . . . And then when he wouldn't sit up they said, . . . "Oh, he's a big baby, he'll sit up." . . . The clinic just ignored me, as much as to say, "You don't know anything about it." (Mother had been a nursery nurse) [Hewett, 1970: 39].

When parents have experiences such as these, they may seek another opinion in order to resolve the conflict between their observations and medical pronouncements to the contrary. Such seeking is sometimes defined by physicians as shopping around for miracle cures and is believed to be based on parental guilt and denial. As Hewett (1970) shows, however, such shopping is sometimes simply based on inaccurate diagnoses:

Mother No. 1 has a mildly handicapped boy of 8; when her son tried to walk at 18 months, he fell frequently. . . . He was referred by the general practitioner to hospital, where the mother was told there was nothing really wrong. He would improve with time and patience. He did not improve. Father then decided it would be worthwhile to pay for a second opinion, and saw a consultant recommended by the general practitioner. A diagnosis of muscular dystrophy was made and the parents told there was no hope of a cure. They were not prepared to believe this and contacted a London hospital, where a diagnosis of cerebral palsy was made after several weeks of investigation with the boy as an inpatient. He was by this time over 3 years old. He began to have physiotherapy and . . . goes to an ordinary day school . . . Who knows what the outcome would have been if the parents had accepted either the original consultant's opinion or the second — their first attempt at "shopping around"? [Hewett, 1970: 184-185]

Thus, at first, the parents of congenitally handicapped children are likely to experience shock, disbelief, and disappointment, and these feelings may not be eased by the professional explanations they receive. Parents are particularly upset by affective neutrality and avoidance on the part of doctors and other professionals and express a need for a sympathetic informant. Professionals have argued that these early definitions are likely to produce hostility toward the child. Thus, in the beginning, these parents are possibly more rejecting than accepting of their defective children. Whether such a response will affect later feelings toward the child is an empirical question, although as suggested in the expectation stated earlier, first responses are likely to be overshadowed by later defintions.

THE POSTPARTUM PERIOD AND LATER INFANCY: ACCEPTING REALITY

McDonald (1971) has noted that professional workers report that period between the diagnosis of a child's handicap and learning what to do about it as being the most traumatic for parents. In his study of paralytic polio convalescence, David (1956) noted that parents' orientations to illness generally involve diseases of short duration, and when faced with an illness with a lengthy period of recovery, they must "redefine the situation." One might expect a similar process of redefinition to be necessary for parents of children with permanently disabling birth defects.

Some parents try to avoid emotional involvement at first because they know that the baby might die: "The doctor said she only had a 50/50 chance and asked me if I wanted to hold her. I didn't after that" (Walker, 1971: 465). Others avoid visiting and handling the baby out of fear:

I saw her on the tenth day. I was terrified of that baby — scared to go and see her. I didn't know whether to expect a monster or not. I couldn't go into the room.

I never held her. She was in an incubator. Sister said to take hold of her hand, but I couldn't.

I was afraid to hold her, but tried to. She was different. I was so scared of that baby. I never thought I would have one like this [Walker, 1971 466].

Psychiatrists have suggested that parents must mourn the loss of their anticipated healthy child before they can love their defective child (see Solnit and Stark, 1961). In the extreme case, the child is defined as intolerable and sent to a foster home or institution. Walker (1971) notes that in a group of parents with spina bifida infants, such rejection is more common among those who lost a spina bifida child previously and "could not go through it again."

In the later stages of the postpartum period, new significant others begin to become more involved in defining the situation for the parents: other children at home, relatives, friends, neighbors, and sometimes social workers or clergymen. The medical "experts" may continue to be salient in those cases in which the child's fate largely rests with them.

A major turning point occurs when the baby finally comes home. Any baby's homecoming occurs in the midst of various situational contingencies such as problems involving siblings or other family members. In the case of the defective baby in particular, these problems are likely to be overshadowed by the entrance of the baby into the family circle.

Parents in one study of myelomeningocele families (Walker, 1971) expressed great concern about handling their babies. Most were told to "treat the baby as normal" but found such treatment to be impossible. They were worried about head injury, damage to the back, and even washing and dressing sometimes caused concern. Because most parents have been separated from their child until this time, the baby's homecoming is the point at which the child begins to become a salient significant other for the parents in most cases. At this time, then, the nature of parent-child interaction begins to become increasingly important in parents' definitions of their children.

The great amount of parental attention that handicapped children elicit is likely to cause problems for the parents' other significant others: the spouse and other children.

Several studies (Walker, 1971; Kolin, 1971; Hare, 1966; Freeston, 1971; Tew et al., 1977) report cases of marital breakdown that appear to be attributable, at least in part, to the handicapped child. However, the great majority of parents have reported that the birth of the child "brought them closer together." Fowle (1968) reports, further, that parents of institutionalized retarded children showed no difference in marital integration from those who kept their children at home. Finally, Dorner (1975) and Martin (1975) present data showing no difference between the divorce rates of parents of children with spina bifida and the rest of the population. The effect on siblings is also variable. In some cases, older children are left to carry out household duties while their parents are at the hospital with the baby. Younger children might be left in the care of strangers at these times. They are also likely to be affected by parental anxiety and remarks made by playmates and others (Walker, 1971). One study (Fowle, 1968) that compared the siblings of severely retarded children who were institutionalized with those whose brothers and sisters were kept at home found that sibling role tension was higher in the noninstitutionalized group, particularly in the case of the oldest female sibling. Older sisters are probably more likely than other children in the family to be recruited to help care for younger retarded siblings. Finally, in a study comparing children with cerebral palsy with their normal twins (Shere, 1956), the handicapped twins were shown to be likely to receive more parental attention and to be better adjusted than their normal siblings. The nonhandicapped twins usually appeared to consider themselves unfairly treated and to be more jealous and less able to control their emotions. Hewett (1970), however, found equal amounts of jealousy in the siblings of the cerebral palsied children she studied and the siblings of a normal group. Further, Caldwell and Guze (1960) found no difference in anxiety between siblings of institutionalized and noninstitutionalized retarded children. Siblings then, *might* issue negative definitions of the baby that might possibly, in turn, influence the parents.

Other significant (and nonsignificant) others also begin defining the child at this time. One study of parents of children with spina bifida (Hare, 1966) found that most parents did not mind people's knowing about the baby's condition and that friends and relatives had all been sympathetic and helpful. Another study, however (Walker, 1971) found that the interest of the neighbors in their spina bifida child was disconcerting to parents. They quote remarks such as the following: "People are beginning to look at this enormous baby lying flat. I'll have to develop a thick skin," and "People are reluctant to look in the pram — they are ignorant about spina bifida — they don't know what to expect." Similarly, a study of parents of children with cystic fibrosis (Meyerowitz and Kaplan, 1967) found that about half of the sample perceived community attitudes as negative and felt some degree of social isolation. The effect of this societal reaction can be strong. Those parents in the study who saw their situation as "impossible" or "embarrassing" were more likely to hospitalize their child, *regardless* of the child's medical condition.

Medical personnel continue to be potential significant others for parents throughout their child's infancy, because both out and inpatient visits are likey to be frequent. Each hospital admission is a potential turning point, in terms of creating new interactional possibilies. Outpatient visits are also likely to bring parents into contact with doctors, nurses, therapists, technicians, and social workers, as well as other parents. In one study (Walker, 1971), mothers of myelomeningocele children expressed concern over the exposure of their child both to parents of normal children and to more severely handicapped children at the clinic. Such exposure produces a threat of negative evaluation of their child.

Alternatively, medical personnel might decrease in significance during the infancy period if they continue to fail to meet the affective needs of parents. As Freidson (1961: 175) has written, "It is my thesis that the separate worlds of experience and reference of the layman and the professional worker are always in potential conflict with each other." Thus, while a mother is likely to view her defective baby as special, for the doctor, "the routine of practice not only makes varied elements of experience equivalent — it also makes them *ordinary*" (Freidson, 1961: 176).

In addition, doctors are typically trained to treat acute illnesses rather than the chronic variety represented by children with birth defects. They have been trained as healers; their basic mission is to cure. A world view that primarily involves sick people who get better may not leave room for the chronically ill or incurable patient, whose defect cannot be "fixed." Medical measures in these cases may improve function but they do not bring about normalcy. Even if spinal surgery is performed on myelomeningocele children, they may still never walk, and a Down's Syndrome baby whose intestinal blockage is relieved will be retarded nonetheless. The rewards, then, for physicians, of treating such patients are perhaps not as great as those stemming from making a baby normal through their actions. One study (Mawardi, 1965) found that when doctors were asked which aspects of their careers they found most satisfying they usually noted "good therapeutic results or a large percentage of successful cases." If success is equated with complete normalcy of function, the chronically ill or disabled represent a form of failure to the physician so oriented. Not surprisingly, then, a study of a small group of pediatricians (Ford, 1967) found that none of the respondents especially liked chronically ill patients, 54% claimed they felt no different toward chronically ill and other patients, and 46% said they disliked the chronic cases. Similarly, in a survey of medical students (Ford, 1967: 22), an "unfavorable orientation was expressed toward demanding, hostile, severely disabled, and hopelessly ill patients."

Thus, if parents accepted the views of their physicians, they might be likely to regard their handicapped children unfavorably. As Freidson (1961) has suggested, however, patients often develop alternative definitions of the situation through interaction in "lay referral structures". Freidson cites the culture and cohesiveness of the structure as major variables in encouraging or preventing physician contact. Thus, a negative evaluation of a child by a physician might not influence parents to define their child similarly *if the lay culture approved* of the child.

Haug and Sussman (1969) suggest a number of grounds on which professional judgments are likely to be questioned by clients: (1) the expertise of practitioners is seen as inadequate, (2) their claims to altruism are seen as unfounded, (3) the organizational delivery system supporting their authority is regarded as defective or insufficient, or, (4) this system is seen as too efficient, exceeding the appropriate bounds of its power. Similarly, Freidson (1961) found that patients expected two qualities in their physicians: (1) technical competence and (2) ability to satisfy emotional needs. Questions about competence in the emotional area were raised more than questions of technical ability. Kuhn (1962) has also noted how professionals lose rapport with their clients by engaging in mystification, including the use of technical jargon. To the extent that professionals are unable to meet the instrumental and socioemotional needs of families of handicapped children, they are likely to lose their significance as evaluators of those children. Thus, Hewett (1970) quotes a mother in her study:

I'm not frightened of (the doctor), not in any way. I speak my mind, I've learned that, all these years of struggling with her and seeing different doctors — you know — and having to fight for the child all the time, which you *do* have to do. Because she can't fight for herself, therefore you have to do it [1970: 46].

Hewett continues:

This was not the only reference to the feeling that parents have to fight for their children, the feeling that doctors (and other professional people) are opponents rather than allies, to be approached with a mixture of caution and militance rather than confidence [1970: 46].

She also notes that parents often got little help and advice from their doctors and that some went to great lengths to get needed services for their children, including one family that wrote to the prime minister.

In a study of four outpatient clinics dealing with chronic pediatric health problems, Powell (1975) showed how the affective needs of families often were not met. In all of the clinics, families tended to talk about home-related issues, while staff focused the conversation on technical, medical problems. Conflict situations resulted in cases where medical recommendations were not appropriate in various individual family settings. As Roth (1962) has noted in another context:

the goals of the professional in his relationship to the client tend to be highly specialized..., whereas the goals of the client include goals generated by all of his roles in addition to that of client of a given professional person [1962: 577].

Powell noted that those families who belonged to voluntary associations concerned with chronic illness were more able to overcome staff resistance and direct the interaction toward their own perceived needs. As Roth (1962) has suggested, the informed client is in a better bargaining position *vis-à-vis* the professional. Thus, association families are probably more likely than others to be able to maintain favorable definitions of their children because of their access to a broader definitional base.

As congenitally handicapped children become integrated into a family, then, parental acceptance is likely to be contingent on a number of situational factors and defining interactions. Important significant others at this time are likely to be the children themselves, siblings, spouses, and other family members, neighbors and friends, members of voluntary associations, and *when supportive of lay definitions*, doctors, nurses, social workers, and other professionals.

CHILDHOOD: CONTINUING INTERACTIONAL ADJUSTMENTS

Parent-child interaction begins to become more patterned in childhood, and the child's level of performance may become increasingly important as a determinant of parental acceptance. Infants are expected to be dependent whether they are normal or handicapped. With time, however, normal children become increasingly independent and, hence, become more differentiated from the retarded and physically impaired. The literature is replete with examples of parents who are unable to cope with children who are markedly abnormal in their development. Many writers are also suspicious of parents who *seem* to be coping well, accusing them of "*over*normalization," "overcompensation," or "well-disguised rejection." Such suspicions are generally related to the psychoanalytically based theories of guilt discussed earlier.

One such "guilt-based" pattern that is commonly described in the literature is "overprotection." Green and Solnit (1964) describe a "vulnerable child syndrome," the symptoms of which include difficulty with separation, infantilization, including overprotection and lack of discipline, bodily overconcern, hypochondria, and school underachievement. While overprotection no doubt exists as a style of child-rearing (among parents of normal as well as handicapped children), many writers assume rather than demonstrate any connection between such a style and parental guilt.⌋

Another pattern that has received attention in the literature is idealization. A classic report of such a case is presented below:

> Of concern is the obsessional and fanatic devotion of a mother to her mentally and physically defective child. ...The neurotic devotion bestowed is more often the expression of the mother's need than a response to her recognition of the defective child's requirements.
>
> A 43-year-old woman...introduced the topic of her family by announcing, "My child is retarded." She then described this child, Mary, minimizing her limitations and exaggerating her capabilities. ...Lurking beneath the philosophic acceptance of reality by the mother was a fantasy — unexpressed, but active. The magic of intensive attention would make Mary grow to be of normal size and sense. ...By dint of unwavering patience and persistence, the patient had been able to toilet train Mary and teach her to make her wishes known in simple sentences. ...She loved the child with a fervor bordering on religious devotion [Forrer, 1959: 59-60].

The assumption is made by the analyst in the case that the behavior and attitudes in question are unrealistic and pathological, possibly, in part, because the case was reported at a time when children like Mary were generally institutionalized at an early age.

In a more recent study, however, Powell (1975: 149-151) takes a "heads-I-win-tails-you-lose" approach in his discussion of a cystic fibrosis clinic. Any interaction initiated by parents toward their child was viewed as an expression of guilt. On the other hand, if parents did not address their children, they were "avoiding" them. When a couple mentioned that their daughter had been selected as a poster girl, they were described as "overcompensating." Powell writes:

> As with the previous family the problem was how to deal with the guilt of the fatal and hereditary illness of the child. This family attempted to cope with the guilt by idealizing the child; this was accomplished by including her within the network of family activities and by making her the center of attention. Through this compensatory action the family diminished its guilt feelings, and the child, by playing the role of idealized person, contributed to this effort [1975: 151].

Interestingly, the forms of parent-child interaction described by Powell in the cystic fibrosis clinic can be found as readily in the other three clinics he discusses. However, because the other clinics do not treat a "fatal and hereditary illness," no assumption of guilt is made. Idealization might simply be a form of parental behavior that occurs among parents (of both normal and handicapped children) for a variety of reasons. Hewett (1970) reports that "guilt feelings" were just as common in a sample of parents of normal 4 years old as in the parents of handicapped children she studied. Worchel and Worchel (1961) found that while parents of retarded children rated their children's normal siblings as better than "most other children," they rated their retarded children as slightly less favorable than most children, and Zuk (1959a) has shown that while most parents overestimate their children's abilities, the parents of the most severely handicapped tend to be more realistic than others. Thus, "idealization" may be even more prevalent among parents of normal children, who have no reason to feel "guilty."

Patterns such as overprotection and idealization are thus viewed as coping mechanisms used by parents to avoid or deny the problems they face in caring for their handicapped children. Farber (1960) suggests that when coping mechanisms fail, a "crisis of role organization" is likely to result. Farber's conclusion is characteristic of the kind of thinking that Ryan (1971) has called "blaming the victim." This type of reasoning suggests that people with problems create their own difficulties. Thus, if a mother has trouble handling her retarded chld, she is defined as experiencing a "role organization crisis." The usual treatment in such a case would involve counseling the mother. An alternative treatment, that did not blame the victim, might involve the provision of day care servides for the child to relieve the mother of her constant burden. The former method implies that the mother's behavior is pathological and needs changing; the latter suggests that she is responding normally to a difficult situation, which needs alleviating.

The victim-blaming ideology permeates much of the literature on families with handicapped children. The fact that such children create numerous problems for their parents has been well documented. These difficulties include: extra work in routine child care tasks such as bathing and dressing (Schonell and Watts, 1956; Holt, 1958), difficulties in finding appropriate educational or training programs (Schonell and Watts, 1956), difficulties in obtaining equipment such as special wheelchairs and car seats (Hewett, 1970), restricted social life (Holt, 1958; Salk, 1972; Wortis and Margolies, 1955; Schonell and Watts, 1956), lack of relaxation and vacations (Schonell and Watts, 1956; Holt, 1958), financial difficulties (Holt, 1958; Salk, 1972), restrictions on freedom of movement, usually resulting from lack of appropriate child care facilities (Holt, 1958; Salk, 1972; Wortis and Margolies, 1955; Schonell and Watts, 1956), effects on parents' health (Holt, 1958), effects on father's job, involving a job change to be near treatment facilities (Schonell and Watts, 1956; Wortis and Margolies, 1955), concern over the child's future (Wortis and Margolies, 1955; Schonell and Watts, 1956), and effect on housing (Salk, 1972). Not all writers use a victim-blaming framework in interpreting these difficulties, but many do.

Holt (1958) writes of his interviews with 201 families in Great Britain, for example:

> In not one of the families I visited did I consider that the parents had made a full emotional adjustment to the problems, and were able to lead a normal life within the community [1958: 748].

Certainly, with all the problems that a severely handicapped child creates, leading a "normal" life would be difficult. Holt seems to suggest that parents' inability to adjust rather than the practical difficulties created by the child's handicap prevents them from participating in community activities.

Other writers reject this view. Wortis and Margolies (1955) argue, for example, that the difficulties faced by parents of cerebral palsied children are more the result of inadequate community resources than of any disturbance or pathology on the part of the parents. They found, in a study of children attending a special school, that although these children created numerous problems for their families, the families that had the fewest difficulties were those who had interested friends and relatives nearby. Conversely, those with the greatest difficulties had been rejected by their friends and relatives and were faced with all the burdens of caring for the child alone. Wortis and Margolies argue that these parents' concerns are realistic given the social context in which they occur.

Similarly, in a study of 50 Australian familes who did not have access to any kind of day care or training program for their retarded children, Schonell and Watts (1956) found that most mothers were "almost desperate" in their plea for some help in raising their children. Most had been actively involved in a search for information about and treatment for their children's conditions. A follow-up study (Schonell and Rorke, 1960) was conducted after a training center for retarded children had been established in the city. Once this source of help became available, most of the mothers reported being much happier and more relaxed. They felt that they had more free time and that they had benefited from talking to other mothers at the center, while their children had learned important social skills. Thus, again, these parents' concerns seemed to be based on realistic rather than neurotic needs, and these concerns diminished once a practical source of help became available.

The absence of pathology in the parents of handicapped children has also been demonstrated directly in a number of studies. Williams (reported in Goodstein, 1960) found no personality difference between parents of normal and parents of cerebral palsied children. Goodstein (1960) had similar results using a sample of parents of children with cleft palates and parents of physically normal children. In a comparison of 60 mothers of cerebral palsied children with 60 mothers of normal children, Boles (1959) found no difference in anxiety, guilt, rejection, unrealistic attitudes, social withdrawal, or expectations for the child between the two groups. He did find significant differences in overprotection, marital conflict, parental evaluaton of the child, and social opportunities for the child. The fact that these children are more sheltered and not seen as favorably as normal children by their parents seems, then, not to have any relationship to guilt or rejection. Rather, parents seem to realistically accept their children's limitations.

Although handicapped children no doubt create problems for their families, in most cases the family seems to adjust to the difficulties. One study of 43 families with Down's Syndrome children (Schipper, 1959) found that two-thirds of the families had integrated the retarded child into family life and that their lifestyle was not significantly changed. Most of the siblings were also happy and well-adjusted, and neighbors were reported to be accepting. The families that were poorly adjusted were those that had serious personal or financial problems in addition to their handicapped child. In those cases, the child sometimes became the straw that broke the camel's back.⌝

Similarly, Hewett (1970) found that mothering patterns were the same in a cerebral palsy group as in a normal population. She concurs in the following description of parents of the handicapped:

> They all seemed to have set about the business of rearing the handicapped child according to whatever set of beliefs they held about child-rearing in general, and few of them changed their basic set of beliefs, even in the face of difficulties encountered in their day-by-day practices [Barsch, 1968, quoted in Hewett, 1970: 113].

In another study, Caldwell and Guze (1960) found no difference in a psychiatric evaluation between mothers who had institutionalized their retarded children and those who had kept their children at home. Both groups seemed to be adjusting well. The mothers also did not differ in their child-rearing attitudes. The authors write:

> The interviewer was impressed by the nearly universal courage, strength, and adaptability of these mothers. There was the general impression that as a result of their experiences nearly all of the women were more sensitive and sympathetic to people with all kinds of problems and handicaps [Caldwell and Guze, 1960: 851].

A number of studies have concluded that the family life of those having a defective child is not significantly different from that of families with normal children (see, for example, Salk, 1972; Birenbaum, 1970, 1971; Voysey, 1975). Few have gone beyond this conclusion to investigate the process by which normalized routines are established. Two writers, however, have focused especially on this process in their studies. They are Birenbaum (1970, 1971) and Voysey (1972, 1975).

Birenbaum (1970) argues that mothers of retarded children attempt to establish a "normal-appearing round of life." He reports (1971) that mothers expressed to him an ideology that entailed treating the retarded child "as normally as possible." Because such treatment is not always feasible, Birenbaum argues that these mothers tend to substitute love, affection, and attention for more instrumental forms of socialization. Because retarded children are typically able to respond emotionally, parents reap greater rewards by stressing the affective aspect of child rearing over intellectual performance or achievement in other areas.

Voysey (1975) explores the problem of normalization in much greater depth, and because of the similarity between her research and that to be undertaken here, her work will be discussed in detail. She begins by differentiating her study from those that assume a pathology framework as well as from those that accept parents' explanations at face value. Her position is one of learning *why* parents use a normality framework in interpreting their own behavior. She argues that parents' actions can be understood from the normative context in which they occur.

Voysey noted that most parents she interviewed claimed that their disabled child had not had a deleterious effect on family life and she became interested in how parents were able to construct such claims. Assuming the perspective of symbolic interactionism, she felt that parents would be likely to define their children in terms provided by others. She writes:

> Basically, I argue that parents' statements on each topic constitute the appearance of normal family life because it is as normal parents that others, both formal and informal agencies, treat them [Voysey, 1975: 27].

Voysey cites four agencies in particular that legitimate parents' claims: religion, medical science, psychiatry, and sociology. Through interaction with these agencies, parents learn that they are not responsible for their child's problem, or that having a disabled child makes a person more mature, or that parents must work to overcome societal ignorance about or stigma toward their children. These rationalizations are supported by voluntary associations that provide models of successful adaptations and magazines and newspapers that print success stories about families of disabled children that are coping well.

Voysey argues that these rationalizations become crystalized in an ideology containing the following elements: (1) acceptance of the inevitable ("It could happen to anyone"), (2) partial loss of the taken-for-granted ("Taking it day to day" — but — "Anything can happen"), (3) the redefinition of good and evil ("There's always someone worse off" or "It's better to know than to be uncertain" or "Death is a blessing" or "We're lucky to be living near good treatment facilities"), (4) the discovery of true values ("At least we've got our health" or "You appreciate your child's progress more when you don't just take it for granted"), (5) the positive value of suffering ("I think I'm more understanding"; "It brings you closer together"), and (6) the positive value of differentness ("It's for his own good"). The development of this ideology is traced, somewhat unsystematically, from the intitial diagnosis of a child's condition to the time of the interview, within a year of the initial diagnosis. Voysey argues that parental definitions are shaped largely by interactions with doctors and with the disabled child.

Voysey suggests that parents employ various techniques of "impression management" in order to sustain their definitions in interactions with others. In "team" performances involving the child, parents may engage in "backstage work" to produce a normal-appearing child. Information control is also practiced. Voysey suggests that parents of the disabled become skilled interactants and good role-takers. In general, "parents of the disabled learn to treat as routine occurrences which embarrass, distress, anger, or otherwise disorient (sic) 'normal' members of society" (1972: 88).

Such interactional techniques were probably relatively unproblematic for many of Voysey's respondents because their children's disabilities were *not visible* to the untrained observer. (The sample included defects such as epilepsy, diabetes, and celiac disease.) On the other hand, no amount of backstage work could make a child with an overwhelmingly obvious disfigurement (a discredited rather than a discreditable condition in Goffman's terms) appear normal. One wonders, then, whether normal appearance is in fact the goal of parents whose children are highly discredited. In these cases, the ideal of realistic acceptance discussed earlier might more accurately describe parents' attitudes and behavior. This possibility is supported by one study of parents and siblings of brain-damaged children (Barsch, 1961) who were quite open and accurate in describing their children's problems to friends and neighbors.

Although highly suggestive, Voysey's study is somewhat limited in scope. The sample included only 19 (only 13 families completed the full series of interviews), mostly blue collar, families in Great Britain, and in most cases, only the mother was interviewed. Because chronic disabilities of all types were included, the ages of the children at the onset of their disabilities were quite variable. This last factor is especially important, because parents might define a child with a defect apparent at birth very differently from one who, having been defined as normal, develops a problem in later childhood or adolescence.

One of Voysey's conclusions seems to contradict the findings of other studies. The primary determinant of parental definitions in Voysey's sample was medical opinion; parents' views were essentially similar to those of their doctors. As noted earlier, however, Freidson (1961) and others have suggested that the professional-client relationship tends to be one of conflict. As Powell (1975), Schonell and Rorke (1960), and others have shown, parents of disabled children are likely to use various lay reference groups who are more supportive than medical personnel and other professionals. Perhaps the parents in Voysey's sample saw their physicians as primary significant others because they were interviewed within a year of the initial diagnosis of their child's problem. At this early stage, other supportive community contacts might not yet be solidified. Most of Voysey's respondents did not belong to parents' organizations or other voluntary associations.

An important research question, then, is: what are the *long-term* definitional consequences of interacting in a stigmatizing society?, and, more specifically, how do the reference sets of parents of handicapped children change over time? What are the important turning points that shape parents' relationships with professionals, friends, relatives, and strangers, as well as with the children themselves? These are the questions that the present study will attempt to answer by employing a career perspective.

Parents' definitions of the situation and of their children, then, are likely to be the emergent products of patterned interactional sequences. At the birth of a handicapped child, parents embark on a career that is likely to be guided at first by the definitions of medical professionals. As conflicts with these professionals and with a stigmatizing society increase, parents' reference sets are likely to shift. A hypothesized pattern of shifting salience based on the literature, is proposed in Table 1. Those parents who finally succeed in coping with their situation are likely to be those who are able to immerse themselves in supportive social networks. These networks, in turn, provide parents with alternative definitions of the situa-

TABLE 1: Hypothesized Salience of Significant Others of Parents of Children with Birth Defects Over Time*

Significant Others	Time in Child's Life Cycle		
	Birth and Postpartum	Infancy	Childhood
Physicians, teachers, and other professionals	*Highly Salient*	Variable salience	May be highly salient if approving; otherwise negatively salient
Family	**Highly salient**	**Highly salient if approving**	**Highly salient if approving**
Friend, neighbors	Variable salience	**Highly salient if approving**	**Highly salient if approving**
The child	Low salience	*Highly salient*	*Highly salient*
Other parents and voluntary associations	Low salience	Moderate salience if available	**Highly salient if available**
The child's peers	Low salience	Low salience	May be moderately salient
Strangers	Low salience	Low salience	Low salience

*Highly salient others are set in boldface type.

The *most* highly salient others at each life cycle point are italicized.

tion to counter societal stigma and victim-blaming. As parents' definitions diverge from those of the professionals who treat their children, however, conflicts are likely to continue.

The primary goal of this study is to discover the processes through which parents of children with serious birth defects establish and maintain positive definitions of their children and of their situation. The research will explore techniques and rationalizations developed by parents over time to overcome the conflicts and hostility of a stigmatizing and victim-blaming society. In many ways, these techniques and rationalizations are likely to be similar to those employed by "deviant" groups of various kinds. As Becker (1963) has suggested, those members of society who are labeled as different are likely to follow a career path leading to the formation of subcultures that justify their existence and repudiate the norms that labeled them. A guiding hypothesis for the following study, then, is that:

parents of disabled children will be successful at maintaining positive definitions of their children and their situation to the extent that they have access to supportive subcultural role models and ideologies.

Such access is probably lowest during the immediate postpartum period and highest during later childhood, perhaps diminishing again in adolescence as the child's interaction experience in various nonsupportive settings increases.

N O T E

1. The terms "fit," "theme," and "revelation" are borrowed from McHugh (1968).

Chapter 3

THE STUDY

Definition of Variables

The problem to be investigated in this study, then, is that of the career paths followed by parents of handicapped children in defining their situation. Parents' role-playing careers will be explored as these relate to changing definitions of the situation. Although handicapped children will not be studied directly, definitions and role-playing by parents are assumed to be the major determinants of children's self-esteem. Thus, the study should help to answer questions about the quality of life of the severely handicapped in American society.

Parents' definitions of the situation at any point in time will include: (1) their definition of their child in cognitive, evaluative, and affective terms, (2) their definition of their relationship with their child, (3) their definition of their relationship with others (both significant and nonsignificant) and the attitudes of those others toward them, (4) their definition of their child's relationship with others in society and the attitudes of those others toward their child, (5) their explanations and rationalizations for the past, present, and future states of their relationships, and their child's relationships, with others and for the attitudes of those others toward them and their child, (6) their definitions of the meaningfulness of the situation, that is, to what degree events and relationships make sense to them, (7) their definitions of power, in terms of their ability to control events and relationships, and (8) their definitions of the normative context, that is, of how closely their definitions of the real situation approximate their conceptions of the ideal. This last component would indicate their relative satisfaction with the existing situation.

The predominant perspective to be taken in the research will be that of the subjects of the study, the parents of handicapped children. As Thomas classically stated, "situations defined as real are real in their consequences." Parents' actions are based on *their perceptions* of events rather than on any absolute reality, and parents' views and actions determine their children's conceptions and attitudes. While the parents' perspective is the most meaningful for the research problem posed here, parents' statements cannot be assumed to be an accurate representation of reality, and Becker (1970) and others have noted the biases inherent in taking the point of view of only one side in a situation. However, some attempt will be made in the research to evaluate the validity of parents' statements with respect to the views of others with whom they are situationally involved.

Parents' definitions, then, will be traced over time. Four time periods will be emphasized as a result of turning points that have been suggested by the literature: (1) the prenatal period: experiences and values held by parents prior to the birth of their child, (2) birth and the immediate postpartum period: initial reactions to the birth of their child and the discovery and diagnosis of the child's problem, (3) later postpartum and infancy: early adjustments to life with a handicapped child, and (4) childhood: continuing adjustments as parents and child interact in a greater variety of social situations. The continuity of these time periods will be assessed in terms of the career perspective described by Becker (1963). The research will attempt to establish patterned sequences of movement from one definitional position to another in terms of the kinds of career contingencies that are likely to arise. Career development generally includes increasing commitments to certain lines of endeavor. However, diversions are likely to occur, making side-tracking possible. A more unlikely, but always possible, outcome is conversion or complete reversal in commitment as a result of various situational contingencies and significant interactions.

In order to control somewhat for the age of the child at the time of diagnosis, only *birth defects* will be considered. Acquired handicaps are thus excluded. In most cases under consideration, then, parents will not have had the opportunity to define their child as normal for very long prior to learning of the child's disability. Birth defects will be further limited to include only disabilities that: (1) are readily apparent (visible) to the lay person and (2) interfere permanently with the child's ability to function in one or more roles consensually defined as normal by society. Thus, only conditions that are clearly stigmatized by the larger society will be considered.

Measurement of Variables

A major component of parents' definition of the situation is their definition of their child. A number of studies have attempted to operationalize this concept. Helper (1958) and Medinnus and Curtis (1963), for example, used a semantic differential, on which parents rated both their real child and their ideal child. Ratings of the real child yielded a measure of parents' evaluations of their children, while differences between real and ideal ratings suggested parental satisfaction with or acceptance of their children. Schwartz and Stryker (1970) argue that the semantic differential is the measure of self and other most appropriate to the symbolic interactionist perspective. Wylie (1974), however, points out that the scales by Osgood et al. that are usually employed in studies using the semantic differential technique were never designed for *self-concept* measurement and therefore do not include all possible *self*-relevant items. The same criticism could be used against the technique as an *other*-rating device.

Another conception of parental acceptance has been used in studies of a more psychologistic nature (Porter, 1954; Hawkes, 1956). Porter (1954: 177) has suggested the following definition:

> *Parental acceptance* may be defined as feelings and behavior on the part of the parents which are characterized by unconditional love for the child, a recognition of the child as a person with feelings who has a right and a need to express those feelings, a value for the unique make-up of the child and a recognition of the child's need to differentiate and separate himself from his parents in order that he may become an autonomous invididual.
>
> *Nonacceptance.* For the purpose of this study, nonacceptance is considered to include rejection, overprotection, indulgence, and other forms of parental behavior which fail to provide the child with an assurance of being a worthy individual who is loved unconditionally and who is respected for his uniqueness and need to become an autonomous individual.

Clearly, such a definition includes certain value-laden notions about child-rearing practices. Two dimensions appear to be involved in the conception: *attitudes* ("unconditional love") and *behavior* ("indulgence"). Attitudes, in turn, seem to include both *evaluations* ("a value for the unique make-up of the child") and *affective states* ("unconditional love for the child"). In addition, the conception involves a general child-view based on the philosophical stance of developmental psychology rather than parents' *definitions* of their children in particular. Defining acceptance in this psychologistic way, accepting parents might *define* their children positively *or* negatively. In other words, such parents love their children whether they think the children are good or bad, intelligent or not intelligent, handsome or homely. Certainly, as studies mentioned earlier indicate, parental love, defined as warmth or interest, is a form of positive definition that contributes to children's self-esteem. However, parental love does not seem to be a sufficient condition for high self-esteem in children. Coopersmith (1967) found, for example, that 57% of the children in his sample with low self-esteem had mothers rated as having considerable or strong affection for them. Thus, if one is searching for a definition of parental acceptance that is meaningful as a determinant of children's self-esteem, one must consider more than affection.

Children who feel loved might still be dissatisfied with their looks, or popularity, or school performance if their significant others define them as lacking in these areas. In addition to defining their children as lovable or not, parents also define them as physically attractive or unattractive, intelligent or unintelligent, well behaved or poorly behaved, kind or cruel, outgoing or shy, generous or selfish, strong or weak. An instrument that purports to measure parents' definitions of children should include definitions in all of the children's important interactional areas. In addition to defining the children in each area, parents will probably also convey to their children whether or not the area itself is *important* to them. Thus, parents who define their children as "not very good-looking" who also teach their children that "looks are not important" might not significantly lower their children's self-esteem with their negative definition.

A number of studies have tried specifically to measure parental conceptions of children with handicaps of various kinds. Some of the psychoanalytically oriented studies noted in the last chapter relied on clinicians' impressions of parental acceptance. Similarly, Zuk (1959a) used the subjective impression obtained from a staff psychiatric social worker at a clinic, a staff pediatrician, or a public health nurse as a measure of parental acceptance of retarded children. Several criteria were established:

> Parents were felt to be acceptant if they: (1) displayed minimal anxiety in the presence of the child or anxiety toward him (2) displayed minimal defensiveness about the child's limitations, and (3) neither obviously rejected the child nor fostered overdependence [Zuk, 1959a: 141].

Such a measure is subject to the bias of the evaluator as well as that of the clinical situation itself. Perhaps what is measured in such a study are the forms of self-presentation used by parents in a clinical setting.

Worchel and Worchel (1961) used an instrument adapted from the Bills' Index of Adjustment and Values, an adjective scale originally designed to measure self-concept. The instrument was used to measure the attitudes of parents toward their mentally retarded children, the concept of the ideal child held by parents, and the attitudes of parents toward most children. The discrepancies between parents' attitudes toward their own child and the ideal child as well as between attitudes toward their own and most children were felt to be measures of acceptance-rejection. Parents in the sample were asked to rate their retarded child as well as one of their child's normal siblings. Discrepancies between real and ideal and between own and most were expected to be greater for the retarded then for the normal child. The use of normal siblings of retarded children as a control group might, however, produce different results from those that would be obtained if normal children *without retarded siblings* were used. Parents might be likely to rate their normal child unusually favorably if their only other child (and basis of comparison) were retarded. The results might be more valid if parents of normal children only were also included as a control group.

Any measure of parental definitions that employs a list of traits forces respondents into defining their children in the terms provided by the instrument. An open-ended measure, on the other hand, would allow parents to define their children *in their own terms*. An open-ended measure was desirable for the present research because the perspective assumed was that of the parents themselves. The instrument used was a modified version of the Kuhn-McPartland Twenty Statements Test (Kuhn and McPartland, 1954), originally designed to measure self-concept. The TST allows respondents to make cognitive and evaluative, as well as affective, statements. Parents were asked to complete four versions of a TST as follows:

(1) (*name of child*) is. . .
(2) If I could have any kind of child (baby) in the world, I would want a child (baby) who was. . .
(3) When (*name of child*) grows up he (she) will probably be. . .
(4) If I could have any kind of child in the world, I would want my child to grow up to be. . .

In each case, the sentence beginning was followed by 20 numbered blank spaces. Parents were thus asked to describe both their real and ideal (an indication of parents' views of the *importance* of various traits) child in the present and in the future, and the degree of correlation between real and ideal was assumed to provide a measure of parental satisfaction.

As a check on and elaboration of TST responses, parents were asked about their definitions of their children at various points during a depth interview. The interview also served as a measure of other aspects of parental definitions of their situation: the nature of relationships with various others, explanations and rationalizations for those relationships, meaningfulness, power, and the normative context. The interview traced definitional change over four time periods: (1) prenatal, (2) birth and early postpartum, (3) later postpartum and infancy, and (4) childhood and adolescence.

The interview also served as a measure of structural conditions and interactional episodes that served as career contingencies in shaping definitional continuity and change. The interview with any one parent was semistructured and lasted from one to five hours. Interview topics were generally derived from the literature and were structured in a chronological sequence beginning with the prenatal period and ending with expectations for the future. The interview thus followed a *modified* life history format, beginning in the immediate prenatal period and continuing to the present. Parents' childhood and early adulthood experiences were only covered to the extent that they related to attitudes toward parenting and toward handicapped children.

The topics covered in the interview included: (1) Background information: child's sex, date of birth, birth defect(s); parent's age, race, original nationality, birthplace, occupation, religion, education, size of·family of origin, marital history, and other children, (2) Prenatal knowledge, attitudes, and experiences: reasons for wanting children, knowledge about and attitudes toward handicapped children, attitudes of significant others, nature of family life and occupational conditions at the time of the pregnancy, (3) Birth: nature of labor and delivery, immediate reactions to the baby, (4) Postpartum: nature of early awareness of the child's problem, early interactions with the child, reactions of other significant others, (5) Infancy: nature of continuing interactions with the child and other significant others, structural conditions such as hospitalizations, and awareness of community stigma, (6) Early childhood: definitions of the child's developmental progress, nursery school experiences, introduction of new significant others such as members of parents' associations, continuing relations with professionals and previous significant others, (7) Later childhood and adolescence: the impact of school entrance and child's increasing interactions with peers, continuing relationship with child and others, and (8) Expectations for the future. The set of questions actually used as guidelines in the interview is included in the Appendix.

The depth interview was selected as the best method for obtaining detailed information and attitudes from parents. The length and relaxed atmosphere of the interview — it was conducted as an extended "conversation" in the subject's home — enabled *process* data to be readily obtained. The lengthy conversational format was also conducive to candid responses.

As a partial correction for recall bias, both mothers and fathers were interviewed. Thus, one parent's version of the past could be compared with that of the other. Differences in recall between parents would not invalidate a study of this type, however, because the parent's own story was in fact the datum being sought in each case. Mother/father differences might highlight the effect of differential sex-linked parental roles on definitions of the situation in the past, present, and future.

Another kind of check on recall bias was the inclusion in the sample of parents of children of various ages. Thus, the birth experience, for example, was related to the interviewer by parents of teenagers and older children as well as by parents of young infants who had just recently given birth. A striking consistency among parents of children of all ages in their definitions of various stages and events was found in the study, suggesting that recollections of the past were probably not grossly distorted among these respondents.

Another potential difficulty of the interview method is impression management. The context of the interview situation and parents' definitions of the interviewer are likely to influence responses. This problem is more likely to arise in interviews of the brief survey type, in which rapport between interviewer and respondent is less likely to develop. Care was taken in the present study to create as much of a backstage atmosphere as possible: Respondents were interviewed in their own homes; the interview was conducted in a conversational style; the parents' anonymity was assured; the interviewer introduced herself as a parent and a student and clearly stated that she was not a doctor. Some impression management no doubt still occurred; however, the interviewer was impressed by the apparent candidness of almost all the respondents. Quite a few parents cried or showed emotion in other ways during the interview. Some thanked the interviewer for listening to their problems and remarked that they welcomed the opportunity to express their feelings. As Merton (quoted in Trice, 1970: 77) has noted:

> informants will not hesitate to make certain private views known to a disinterested outside observer — views which would not be expressed were it thought that they would get back to the management; the outsider has "stranger" value.

In addition to interviewing mothers and fathers separately, several other methods of gauging bias and impression management were employed. First of all, as noted earlier, parents were asked to complete a series of written forms corresponding to some of the material covered in the interview. Discrepancies between written and verbal statements provided one check on the reliability of parents' responses. Validity could also be assessed to some extent by checking written case records on each family and by questioning the nurse who knew the families about individual cases. Finally, a small sample of pediatricians was interviewed to see if their perspective of the doctor-patient relationship matched that of the parents.

Again, differences of viewpoint between parents and professionals would not invalidate the study. Various role-players in a situation will necessarily have different viewpoints as a result of their differential socialization and consequent expectations. Understanding the sources and degree of such differing definitions was in fact an important goal of the study. Getting another perspective, then, was a way of clarifying the parents' perspective; in order to understand how parents arrive at their version of the truth, one should first determine what their version *is* and how their version differs from the versions of others who have participated in the same situations.

Procedure

The study was conducted with the cooperation of the Genetic Counseling Service of a university medical school in a northeastern urban area. The service was a logical source of cases because its clientele included parents who, having already had one or more congenitally handicapped children, were seeking counseling prior to undertaking another pregnancy. In some cases, parents were not contemplating another pregnancy, but counseling was sought because parents were concerned about the genetic consequences for the future offspring of their normal children. In addition to self-referred clients, many had been sent to the service by their obstetricians, pediatricians, or family doctors to obtain more information about their children's defects, whether or not they planned any further pregnancies. The service itself, which was administered by a pediatrician-geneticist and a nurse-associate, had recently evolved from a specialized agency that offered genetic analyses for area physicians to a full-service operation that followed the progress of families after their initial counseling sessions and assisted them in locating various community resources for their children. Thus, both the pediatrician and the nurse-associate had extended personal contact with a large number of their clients.

THE SAMPLE OF PARENTS

The researcher was given complete access to the files of the Genetic Counseling Service. In order to define the population for study, she scanned every case folder and recorded all those that met the following criterion: an intact family containing at least one living, noninstitutionalized child, aged newborn to 19 years, with a serious birth defect.[1] The families of 53 children met this criterion. Each was assigned a number, and, using a table of random numbers, the families of 25 children were selected for inclusion in the study sample. Some substitutions were made in an attempt to stratify the sample somewhat in terms of the age of the children included. Otherwise, the sample would have been heavily composed of families of children of preschool age.

Each of these randomly selected families was sent an introductory letter about the research project signed by the director of the Genetic Counseling Service. The researcher telephoned each family shortly after they had received the letter to make an appointment for an interview.

Several sample substitutions became necessary in the course of the telephoning. Two families had moved, and in another case, the mother had recently died. Only four families refused to be interviewed, and no pressure was exerted to make them change their minds. Because the study was not intended to yield statistical data that could be extrapolated to any given population, a completely representative sample was not deemed essential. The researcher did discuss the noncompliant families with the staff at the Genetic Counseling Service, and in all four cases, the staff judged these families as not having any known significant problems different from those of the families that did comply. One noncompliant mother claimed that she did not "believe in research." Two others said that they did not wish to undergo a potentially stressful interview, and the fourth claimed never to have received the introductory letter and refused to talk to the researcher. In each of these cases, the family of a child of similar age was randomly selected from the population as a substitute. Thus, the final sample contained the desired number — 25 — of cases. The composition of the sample in terms of child's sex, age, defect, socioeconomic status, religion, ethnicity, and family size is presented in Table 2. (All respondents were white.) Some of the defects represented are extremely obvious and incapacitating, as in the case of a 9-and-a-half-year-old child who looks very unusual and is unable to walk, talk, or perform most functions. At the other extreme is a child with an artificial eye that is noticeable, but not glaringly obvious. Her function is essentially normal, and the researcher wonders, in retrospect, if her defect was perhaps not serious enough after all to have been included in the sample. Almost all of the other defects represented were *very* obvious and involved a moderate to high degree of psychomotor retardation.

All of the parent interviews were conducted during a five-month period from September 1976 through January 1977. The same general procedure was followed in each case. The researcher began by having the parents sign a consent form. The form reiterated the aims of the study and briefly presented the procedure to be followed. The study was described as being potentially helpful to professionals in understanding the problems faced by congenitally handicapped children and their parents. The parents were then told that the study had both a written and an oral part and they were asked to decide which parent would do the oral part first. The researcher explained that the oral part (the interview) would take longer than the written part (the TST) but that each parent would be doing both. The parent doing the

TABLE 2: Composition of the Family Sample

Case Number	Child's Sex	Child's Age	Child's Defect	Approximate SES* (UM = upper middle class LM = lower middle class UL = upper lower class)	Religious Background (C = Catholic P = Protestant J = Jewish)	Ethnicity	Number of Living Siblings (O = older Y = younger)
1	M	1 mo.	Down's Syndrome[1]	UM	C	Irish	5 (O)
2	F	1 mo.	,,	U(?)M	C	Belgian/ Italian	1 (O)
3	F	2 mo.	,,	LM	C	Italian/ Irish	0
4	M	10 mo.	,,	UL	C/P	Irish/ English	0
5	M	17 mo.	,,	L(?)M	C/P	Irish/ English	2 (O)
**6	F	2 yrs.	Apert's Syndrome[2]	LM	C	Italian/ Polish	0
7	F	2 yrs.	cerebral palsy	U(?)M	C	Irish/ Polish	0
8	M	2 yrs.	Down's Syndrome	UM	P	Scottish	1 (O)

TABLE 2: Continued

					C/P		
9	F	2½ yrs.	retinoblastoma[3]	LM		Italian/English	1 (O)
**10	M	2½ yrs.	Down's Syndrome	UM	none	English	1 (O)
**11	F	3 yrs.	"	UL	C	French	1 (Y)
12	F	4 yrs.	Cornelia de Lange Syndrome[4]	UM	C	Italian/English	1 (Y)
13	F	4½ yrs.	cataracts	UM	P/J (nonpracticing)	German/Russian	0
14	F	5 yrs.	multiple deformities; psychomotor retardation	LM	C (nonpracticing)	French	0
15	F	6 yrs.	myelomeningocele-hydrocephalus	LM	P	Czech/English	0
16	F	6½ yrs.	Down's Syndrome	LM	C	Polish/Irish	3 (O)
17	M	6½ yrs.	cerebral palsy mentally retarded	UM	C	Irish	1 (O)
18	F	7 yrs.	mentally retarded	UM	C	Irish	2 (O&Y)
19	M	9½ yrs.	multiple deformities; gross psychomotor retardation	LM	P	Scottish/English	2 (O)
20	F	10 yrs.	Down's Syndrome	LM	P	German/English	2 (O&Y)
21	F	12 yrs.	cerebral palsy-like syndrome; legally blind	UL	C	French/Italian	4 (O)

TABLE 2: Continued

				LM	P		
**22	M	13 yrs.	Marfan's Syndrome[5]		P	French/American	2 (O&Y)
23	M	15 yrs.	cerebral palsy-like syndrome; legally blind	UL	C	French/Italian	4 (O&Y)
24	F	18 yrs.	"	"	"	"	"
25	M	19 yrs.	"	"	"	"	"

Cases 21, 23, 24, and 25 are siblings.
*Based on father's occupation, parents' education, and interviewer's judgment
**Mother only participated

1. "Mongolism." A chromosome defect producing unusual appearance, small stature, and (generally) moderate mental retardation.
2. Involves unusual appearance including deformities of the head, hands, and feet. May involve mild to moderate mental retardation.
3. A malignant tumor of the eye(s).
4. A rare, usually fatal, defect involving extremely small stature, unusual appearance, and severe psychomotor retardation.
5. A defect involving unusual appearance, coronary, and often visual difficulties.

96

written part first was asked to leave the room while the other parent was being interviewed. Sometimes, mothers were interviewed first; in other cases, fathers were interviewed first. At the completion of the first interview, parents changed places. In one or two cases, the researcher was not successful in keeping the parents in separate rooms for the entire evening. In these cases, the mother and father were interviewed jointly for brief periods of time. In four cases, only the mother participated. In three of these, the father was unable to be present at the time, and in the fourth, the father refused to participate. All of the interviews were recorded on tape.

Interview times varied considerably. As might be expected, the interview length was generally correlated with the age of the child. The mothers' interviews tended to be a little longer than the fathers', although some of the longest interviews obtained were with fathers. The shortest interview with any one parent lasted about a half hour; the longest took almost five hours. Most ranged from one-and-a-half to three-and-a-half hours.

In all cases but one, the handicapped child was present in the home during the interview. Usually, the child was introduced to the researcher and interacted with her for awhile before going to bed (most of the interviews were conducted in the evening). In most cases, then, the researcher had some opportunity to observe briefly the quality of parent-child interaction.

THE "CONTROL GROUP"

While the study was not intended as an experiment or a rigorously controlled comparison, the researcher felt that testing the instruments on a few parents of only normal children might be helpful. Real/ideal child comparisons on the TST, for example, might be more meaningful if analyzed in conjunction with similar comparisons by parents whose children were not handicapped. Ideally, a large-scale matched study of normals would have been undertaken. Because the research was being conducted by only one person within a definite time limit such a procedure was not possible. However, a token attempt was made to obtain at least a few comparison interviews and TST responses from parents of normal children.

The token sample consisted of only five families, and was a rather biased group in terms of social class and interest in children: all were members of a local organization promoting childbirth and child-rearing education. All were professional families, and in two cases, the father was a physician. The children in these families ranged in age from 1 month to 8 years. Thus, this group cannot be regarded as a matched control group in any sense. Rather, their responses should be viewed as suggestive of possible lines of future research in this area.

THE PEDIATRICIAN SAMPLE AND INTERVIEW

The parents of congenitally handicapped children must interact with a number of community agencies, including professionals such as physicians and educators as well as various lay groups. Usually, though, their earliest and most sustained contact during their child's life cycle tends to be with one or more pediatricians. The pediatrician is usually responsible for first informing parents that their child has a birth defect and often becomes defined as the person responsible for guiding parents along the course they take in child rearing postnatally. Thus, the pediatricians's viewpoint seemed to be the logical one to pursue in obtaining a representation of the definitions of those others in society with whom parents must interact.

A sample of 15 pediatricians was randomly drawn from a list of all pediatricians in private practice in the area covered by the study. Substitutions were then randomly made so that, in the case of group practices, only one physician in any one group was included. Thus, although only 15 physicians were selected from a list of 54, almost all of the group practices in the area were represented. The researcher hoped to obtain at least a fair cross section of medical philosophies in this manner.

Of the 15 pediatricians initially contacted, only one refused to be interviewed, claiming a lack of time. Another pediatrician in a similar solo practice situation was then substituted.

Like the parents, the pediatricians were initially contacted by means of a letter from the director of the Genetic Counseling Service, explaining the purpose of the research. In this case, the director was a colleague of the physicians being contacted, a fact that probably encouraged their cooperation. The letter was followed by a telephone call by the researcher, during which an interview appointment was made.

All of the interviews were conducted in the pediatricians' offices, generally during a lunch hour, or before or after patient appointments for the day. Because of the structure of the situation, these interviews tended to be considerably shorter than those with the parents. The shortest interview took about a half hour, the longest about two hours. Most lasted roughly 45-75 minutes.

As in the parent interviews, the researcher began by asking each pediatrician to read and sign a consent form explaining the purpose of the study and assuring anonymity. The doctors were then interviewed in a somewhat structured manner. A standard form was completed by the researcher in the course of the interview and included such background information as the physician's age, sex, birthplace, marital status, parental status, original nationality, religion, length of practice, medical training, and the presence of birth defects in the physician's own family. The remainder of the interview focused on two issues: (1) the situation of first informing parents that their child has a birth defect and (2) the desirability of treating children with serious birth defects in everyday practice. Both of these issues had been cited by parents as key conflict areas in parent-physician interaction. (A complete copy of the pediatrician interview form appears in the Appendix.)

An important consideration in an interview of this type is impression management by the respondents. However, in almost all cases, these doctors seemed very frank and open. Many readily admitted their distaste for treating the severely handicapped, with candor to a degree that even surprised the interviewer. Most seemed eager to expound on their personal philosophies about birth defects, and many digressed considerably from the established topics of the interview. A few voiced strong opinions on questions such as euthanasia and institutionalization.

All of the interviews, both with parents and with pediatricians, were conducted by one person, a 30-year-old female. The interviewer tried to be as nondirective as possible and never expressed an opinion on any subject. The interviewer's age and sex may have influenced her respondents in some way, although mothers' and fathers' responses — one indication of possible sex-role influence — did not differ significantly. A replication of the study by a different interviewer might be interesting, however, as a control for possible interviewer effect.

NOTE

1. As suggested earlier, "serious birth defect" was defined to include any pre- or perinatal condition that (1) would be apparent to a layperson observing a child so affected and (2) permanently interfered with normal role performance to some degree. Completely correctible conditions (some heart problems, for example) and relatively invisible defects (minor deformities, or diseases such as cystic fibrosis) were thus excluded. The researcher's impressions of visibility and functional impact were checked in questionable cases against those of the nurse-associate who knew the families well.

Chapter 4

PARENTS' DESCRIPTIONS OF THEIR CHILDREN: REALISTIC ACCEPTANCE

In general, most of the parents in the study expressed positive attitudes toward their handicapped children. Their acceptance was not unqualified, however. Many noted periods in the past when they were not completely accepting. In most cases, acceptance seemed to be the outcome of an interactional sequence in which the children themselves became major significant others. Generally, acceptance was realistic: children were valued *in spite of* their limitations. Only a few parents — all of them fathers — seemed to disbelieve the serousness and/or permanence of their child's handicap. These fathers were probably more guilty of lack of knowledge than of denial, however, for they seemed to be unaware of normal developmental milestones in childhood.

Realistic acceptance was expressed verbally in the interview and in written form on the TST. As Table 3 indicates, the child's handicap is generally *not* the most salient feature noted by parents. Although 53% of the parents used "retarded," "handicapped," or a similar term at some point in describing their child on the TST, only 10% mentioned it as

TABLE 3: Salience of Mention of Defect on the RP* Form and of "Normal" on the IP* Form of the TST by Mothers and Fathers

	RP						IP					
	Mention of "retarded," "handicapped," etc. or specific defect						Mention of "normal," "nonhandicapped," etc.					
	Mothers		Fathers		Total		Mothers		Fathers		Total	
Salience Mentioned as :	n	%	n	%	n	%	n	%	n	%	n	%
1 or 2	2	(9)	2	(12)	4	(10)	14	(64)	8	(47)	22	(56)
3 or 4	6	(27)	3	(18)	9	(23)	1	(4)	2	(12)	3	(8)
5-10	3	(14)	3	(18)	6	(15)	1	(4)	1	(6)	2	(5)
11-20	1	(4)	1	(6)	2	(5)	0	(0)	0	(0)	0	(0)
Not mentioned	10	(45)	8	(47)	18	(46)	6	(27)	6	(35)	12	(31)
Total	22	(100)	17	(100)	39	(100)**	22	(100)	17	(100)	39	(100)

**The parents of four handicapped children (cases 21, 23-25) completed the TST for only one of their children (case 12) had to leave his home during the evening. He was interviewed but never completed the TST forms.

*The following abbreviations will be used for the four forms of the TST: RP ("Real Present"); IP ("Ideal Present"): "———— is:"; 21); in addition, one father who participated in the study "When ———— grows up . . ."; IF ("Ideal Future"): "If I could have . . . my child to grow up to be:" is:"; IP ("Ideal Present"): "If I could have . . . a child who was:"; RF ("Real Future"):

the first or second item on their list, even though they were aware that the present study was concerned with birth defects. Next, 23% mentioned in third or fourth, 15% from fifth to tenth, 5% between eleventh and twentieth, and 46% did not mention it at all. Thus, although parents do not generally deny their child's defect, neither do they see it as the prime or only attribute their child has.

Even though parents see their children as being more than merely handicapped or retarded, if given a choice, they would not want their children to bear such afflictions. The desirability of having a normal child is evidenced by the fact that 56% of the parents mentioned "normal" as the *first or second* item on the ideal child form. As Table 3 indicates, "normal" was both highly salient and highly mentioned: 69% of the parents listed "normal," "nonhandicapped," or a similar term somewhere on the form. Thus, although parents do not necessarily reject their handicapped children, they would certainly prefer to have had children who were normal. This finding tends to refute the psychoanalytically based notion that parents defensively idealize their handicapped children.

Interestingly, most of the parents in the token "control group" also listed "normal" on the ideal child form. This finding should be regarded cautiously, however, because these parents were aware, when filling out the forms, that the study included a sample of parents of children with birth defects. Even without this awareness, though, "normal" might have been a likely response. In American culture, when expectant parents are asked about the desired sex of their anticipated offspring, they typically reply, "It doesn't matter, as long as the baby is healthy." Health and normality may thus be salient ideals for all parents whether their real children are normal or handicapped.

While most parents of handicapped children recognize their children's failings, then, they also define their offspring

TABLE 4: Ratio of Consensual to Subconsensual Responses on RP Form of the TST by Mothers and Fathers of Handicapped and Nonhandicapped Children

| | Parents of Children with Birth Defects | | | |
| **Mothers** | **(n = 22)** | | **Fathers** | **(n = 17)** |
C/S Ratio		% consensual responses	C/S Ratio		% consensual responses
10:1	=	91	2:0	=	100
5:2	=	71	7:3	=	70
14:6	=	70	2:1	=	67
3:2	=	60	1:1	=	50
6:4	=	60	10:10	=	50
7:5	=	58	3:4	=	43
8:7	=	53	6:8	=	43
10:10	=	50	8:12	=	40
3:4	=	43	1:2	=	33
4:6	=	40	1:2	=	33
4:6	=	40	2:5	=	29
4:6	=	40	3:8	=	27
7:13	=	35	3:8	=	27
1:2	=	33	2:10	=	17
4:9	=	31	1:6	=	14
4:9	=	31	2:18	=	10
4:9	=	31	0:5	=	0
1:4	=	20			
1:4	=	20			
2:13	=	13			
2:18	=	10			
0:5	=	0			

Mean = 40.91% consensual   Mean = 38.41% consensual
Median = 40% consensual   Median = 33% consensual

Mean = 39.82% consensual   Median = 40% consensual σ = 22.6

TABLE 4: Continued

Parents of Normal Children

Mothers (n = 5)		Fathers (n = 5)	
C/S Ratio	% consensual	C/S Ratio	% consensual
14:6 = 70		14:6 = 70	
9:11 = 45		9:11 = 45	
9:11 = 45		4:16 = 20	
6:14 = 30		2:15 = 12	
5:15 = 25		0:15 = 0	

Mean = 43% consensual
Median = 45% consensual

Mean = 29.4% consensual
Median = 20% consensual

Mean = 36.2% consensual   Median = 37.5% consensual   σ = 22

in terms of their various other attributes, both consensual and subconsensual. As Table 4 indicates, the ratio of consensual to subconsensual responses varies considerably from one parent to another. Consensual responses included statements such as "_____ is retarded," "_____ has brown hair," "_____ is a grandson," "_____ is five years old," among others. Some typical subconsensual responses are given below:

_____ is:

warm (M*)

mischievous (M)

stubborn (F**)

inquisitive (M)

fun to play with (M)

my little love (M)

burdensome to parents in that plans evolve around her (F)

a binding force in the family as a whole (F)

a joy to me and her family (M)

retarded but can learn (M)

a beautiful child (M)

special gift (F)

a challenge (F)

a teacher to all of us (F)

unhappy with his body but likes his brain (M)

very important in my life (M)

very good natured (M)

the most precious child in the world (M)

very much liked by her teachers (M)

a happy child with CP (F)

willing to learn (F)

a very loving child (F)

playful (M)

always busy (M)

difficult to take places at times (M)

frustrated by many things (M)

   * Statement made by mother.

 ** Statement made by father.

Most of the RP forms included both positive and negative subconsensual statements, although the positive tended to predominate. The following complete forms are illustrative. The first is from the mother of a child with an extremely severe psychomotor handicap, the second from the father of a Down's Syndrome child. (The names have been changed in both cases.)

Who is Billy?

Billy is:

1. my child
2. my youngest

3. my baby
4. has lots of handicaps
5. stubborn but cute when he is
6. unable to walk
7. heavy
8. funny
9. skinny
10. bald but used to have beautiful hair
11. always trying
12. sick sometimes
13. always with us
14. always liking me
15. hurting but can't tell me
16. brave
17. a good boy
18. tired
19. a person
20. worth it

Who is Joey?

Joey is:
1. small
2. curious
3. lovable
4. a boy
5. a brother
6. a son
7. retarded
8. enlightening
9. normal to care for
10. has special educational needs

11. special

12. a joy to his sister, mom and dad

13. loved

14. human

15. accepted

16. 2 years old

17. developing slowly but surely

18. a baby

19. a teacher of compassion and love

20. hope

Birenbaum (1971) has argued that parents of retarded children are able to accept their children more readily because they substitute the socioemotional or expressive attributes ("love") that their children possess for the more instrumental attributes ("intelligence," "success") found in normal children. The date of Table 4 do not entirely support Birenbaum's argument. Although subconsensual statements do predominate on most parents' lists, the average form still contained about 40% consensual statements. In the small check sample of parents of normal children, only about 36% of the statements made on the average form were consensual. Thus, although the check sample used was definitely not an adequate control group, the results tend to suggest that *all* parents define their children more in subconsensual than in consensual terms. These findings should certainly be checked against a more broadly based (especially in terms of education and socioeconomic status) sample of parents of normal children.

Subconsensual responses predominated to an even greater extent on the ideal child forms. Some typical IP responses follow:

If I could have any kind of child in the world, I would want a child who was:

polite

happy

kind

loving

healthy

intelligent

attractive

well-liked

honest

friendly

some children with the personality that _____ (respondent's
handicapped child) has

God-fearing

charitable

lovable

as normal as possible even if handicapped

good-natured

good

loved

easy to care for

someone to be proud of

did not have to experience great pain

did not always have to be different

did not always have to fight to live

Thus, cognitive or consensual characteristics such as sex or
physical appearance do not seem to be as important to
parents as various personal-social traits that suggest acceptance by others. In general, most parents painted a picture of
an ideal child who was *socially* normal: one who was
unselfish, cooperative, loved, and respected.

How closely do the real children approximate their parents'
ideal? Table 5 indicates the percentage of ideal responses
found in parents' descriptions of their real child. On the

④

TABLE 5: Percentage of IP Responses Also Appearing on RP Forms of Mothers and Fathers of Handicapped and Nonhandicapped Children

Parents of Children with Birth Defects

Mothers	(n = 22)	Fathers	(n = 17)
100%	(1/1)	100%	(1/1)
60	(3/5)	67	(2/3)
50	(1/2)	40	(2/5)
40	(2/5)	33	(1/3)
40	(2/5)	33	(1/3)
35	(7/20)	33	(1/3)
33	(1/3)	29	(4/14)
25	(2/8)	25	(5/20)
20	(1/5)	25	(3/12)
14	(1/7)	20	(2/10)
11	(1/9)	5	(1/20)
8	(1/13)	0	(0/3)
8	(1/13)	0	(0/4)
0	(0/3)	0	(0/1)
0	(0/3)	0	(0/5)
0	(0/4)	0	(0/9)
0	(0/1)	0	(0/4)
0	(0/4)		
0	(0/11)		
0	(0/7)		
0	(0/4)		
0	(0/1)		
Mean = 20.18%		Mean = 24.12%	
Median = 9.5		Median = 25	

Mean = 21.9%   Median = 14% $\sigma = 25.9$

Parents of Normal Children

Mothers	(n = 5)	Fathers	(n = 5)
30%	(6/20)	43%	(3/7)
27	(3/11)	40	(8/20)
25	(5/20)	20	(4/20)
20	(2/10)	6	(1/17)
5	(1/20)	5	(1/20)
Mean = 21.4%		Mean = 22.8%	
Median = 25%		Median = 20%	

Mean = 22.1%   Median = 22.5% $\sigma = 13.06$

average, only about 22% of the items on the real child form overlapped those on the ideal form. Further, 14 parents (about 36% of the sample) saw *no correspondence* between their real and ideal child. One should not necessarily assume, however, that the lack of correspondence results from the fact that these children are handicapped. Indeed, in the small check sample of parents of normal children, the average real-ideal correspondence was also only about 22%. Perhaps then, *most parents* do not come close to having what they would define as the perfect child.

The lack of real-ideal correspondence should also not be taken to mean that these parents do not love or accept their children. Indeed, most parents would prefer that their children were normal and healthy *because* they love them and do not like to see the children suffer stigma and pain. Such an interpretation becomes especially feasible in light of the interview data to be presented later.

Although the overall correspondence between real and ideal is low, this finding might be an artifact of the nature of the test. Parents might include in a long list of ideal attributes qualities that they do not value highly. The ideal form encourages parents to list aspirations that might not be realistic expectations even if their child were normal. Thus, a parent might *aspire* to have a genius, but most parents do not *expect* their children to be geniuses and are quite content to have a child of reasonable intelligence.

One way of controlling for unrealistic aspirations to some extent is to focus only on parents' most salient responses on the ideal form. Table 6 shows the degree of correspondence between the real child forms and the *first three* items listed on the ideal form. Presumably, parents list the traits that are most important to them at the outset before they indulge in greater degrees of fantasy. Using only these highly salient items, 54% of the parents had no real-ideal correspondence, while 46% showed a correspondence with at least one of the

TABLE 6: The Percentage of Mothers and Fathers of Handicapped and Nonhandicapped Children Indicating Various Degrees of Correspondence Between the RP and the Most Salient Items on the IP Forms of the TST

Parents of Children With Birth Defects

	Mothers		Fathers		Total	
	n	%	n	%	n	%
No correspondence (0/3, 0/2, 0/1)	11	(50)	10	(59)	21	(54)
Low correspondence (1/3)	8	(36)	5	(29)	13	(33)
Moderate correspondence (2/3 or 1/2)	2	(9)	1	(6)	3	(8)
High correspondence (3/3, 2/2, 1/1)	1	(5)	1	(6)	2	(5)
Total	22	(100)	17	(100)	39	(100)

Parents of Normal Children

	Mothers	Fathers	Total	
	n	n	n	%
Correspondence None	1	1	2	(20)
Low	2	2	4	(40)
Moderate	2	1	3	(30)
High	0	1	1	(10)
Total	5	5	10	(100)

most salient ideal items. Thus, slightly less than half of the parents define their handicapped children as conforming in at least one respect with what they believe to be important and desirable qualities in a child.

In the small check sample of parents of normal children, fully *80%* saw a similar correspondence between their real and ideal child. These findings suggest that normal children do come closer to approximating the *most salient* ideal traits as perceived by their parents. Further research on parents of normal children would certainly be desirable to substantiate this finding.

Even though children might approximate their parents' ideals *as children*, they might not grow up to be the kind of adults their parents would desire. Particularly in the case of severely handicapped children, parents must accept the fact that their children may never play normal occupational, marital, and parental roles. Indeed, most parents of handicapped children in the sample did express normal role aspirations on the ideal form. The following responses are illustrative:

If I could have any kind of child in the world, I would want my child to grow up to be:

independent	healthy
a good person	intelligent
a loving wife	charitable
a caring mother	loving
successful	sincere
happy	hard working
respected	responsible
owner of a sheet metal shop	a doctor
well adjusted	prosperous
whatever she wants to be	well-educated
having healthy children	a Christian
a professional person	family-oriented

In contrast, the following responses were typical of the parents in the sample with respect to their expectations for their real child:

When _____ grows up, he (she) will probably be:
able to care for his personal needs
happy
a good housekeeper
working in a sheltered workshop
well liked by her associates
not very intelligent
made fun of by people
as capable as a 10 year old
a loving companion for us
my pal
not very tall
friendly
polite
able to care for himself to a certain degree
a child in mind and heart
slow
kind
loved
unusual in appearance
don't know what to expect
lovable
not married
dependent on us
a happy-go-lucky old maid
a very neat person
a doting aunt

TABLE 7: Percentage of IF Responses Also Appearing on RF Forms of Mothers and Fathers of Handicapped and Nonhandicapped Children

Parents of Children With Birth Defects

Mothers	(n = 20*)	Fathers	(n = 14*)
100%	(2/2)	100%	(1/1)
50	(1/2)	80	(16/20)
40	(8/20)	50	(1/2)
37.5	(3/8)	33	(1/3)
27	(3/11)	14	(2/14)
25	(2/8)	12.5	(1/8)
20	(1/5)	10	(1/10)
11	(1/9)	5	(1/20)
7	(1/14)	0	(0/4)
0	(0/4)	0	(0/4)
0	(0/5)	0	(0/8)
0	(0/5)	0	(0/1)
0	(0/8)	0	(0/3)
0	(0/8)	0	(0/13)
0	(0/5)		
0	(0/20)		
0	(0/2)		
0	(0/12)		
0	(0/7)		
0	(0/5)		
Mean = 15.9%		Mean = 21.75%	
Median = 0		Median = 7.5%	

Mean = 18.29%   Median = 10.5% $\sigma = 27.93$

Parents of Normal Children

Mothers	(n = 4*)	Fathers	(n = 5)
60%	(12/20)	37.5%	(3/8)
38	(5/13)	35	(7/20)
33	(2/6)	20	(4/20)
20	(4/20)	15	(3/20)
		13	(2/15)
Mean = 37.75%		Mean = 24.1%	
Median = 35.5%		Median = 20%	

Mean = 30.17%   Median = 33% $\sigma = 14.02$

*Three fathers and two mothers in the study sample and one mother in the "control group" felt they could not even guess about their child's future and did not complete the RF form.

Table 7 shows the correlation between parents' aspirations and expectations for the future. On the average, parents listed only about 18% of the items on the ideal form on the real form as well. Further, 17 parents (50% of the sample) had no correlation at all between the two forms. Thus, parents' projections for the future are slightly further from their ideal than their idea of the present.

In the check sample of parents of normal children, on the other hand, projections for the future *come closer* to parents' ideals than their idea of the present: the average parent saw a 22% correlation between their real and ideal child in the present and a 30% correlation between their real and ideal child in the future. Of course, most parents still do not envision their child's developing into what they see as the perfect adult. Some, however, seem to feel, optimistically, that although their child has some faults, future socialization will bring the child closer to their ideal. Such optimism does not seem to be present in the case of the parents of the handicapped.

The results appear to support the ideology of living day to day described by Voysey (1975). Parents of handicapped children are probably likely to rely on a present time orientation because the future is bleak, or uncertain at best. However, as shown above, many parents *do* seem to be able to anticipate their child's adulthood favorably. Such a positive outlook seems to be accomplished by finding pleasure in some real role the child will be able to play rather than by dwelling on roles that are unattainable. Thus, a number of parents stressed the companionship role, seeing the children as future "pals" even after their siblings have left home. Others emphasized the continuation of family ties on a visitation basis if they saw the child as part of a group home, halfway house, or other sheltered environment. As the interview data will later indicate, most parents were very concerned about the possibility that their child might eventually be institutionalized. None of the parents was pessimistic enough to include the idea of certain institutionalization on the RF form, however.

Real-ideal discrepancies may not indicate anything about parental acceptance. In perusing the lists of parents with high and low real-ideal correspondence, the researcher could not detect any meaningful differences between the lists in background traits, career experiences, or apparent acceptance, as revealed by the interview data. Typically, the mother and father of the *same child* were very different in degree of real-ideal correspondence on the TST, indicating that parents' subjective impressions, and not the child's objective condition, are important in shaping test responses. Such variations in wishful thinking do not seem to be correlated with attitudes toward the real child. Many define their handicapped children as being quite far from ideal, but such a definition may not indicate anything about the parents' ability to love, nurture, and accept such children despite their shortcomings. Some of the parents with the lowest real-ideal corespondence had children with the most severe handicaps. Typically, these parents were bitter and disappointed *for their children's sake*. They were upset that their children had to suffer but were still able to enjoy their offspring and to attempt to provide the best possible life for them under the circumstances. If not totally accepting, they were, at least, *committed* to their children and to their welfare. The development of such commitments will be explored more fully in the next chapter.

In general, mothers as a whole and fathers as a whole responded similarly on the TST, although some sex-role patterned differences did emerge. For the most part, fathers tended to be *slightly* more optimistic or idealistic than mothers: fathers were slightly less likely to mention "normal" on the IP form (see Table 3); they made fewer consensual statements on the RP form (see Table 4), and their real and ideal descriptions were more closely correlated, both in the present and in the future (see Tables 5 and 7). (As Table 6 indicates, however, mothers had a very slightly higher real-ideal correlation for the *most salient* ideal items in the present.)

The slight tendency of fathers to idealize their children may result from their relative lack of relevant interactional experience. Generally, mothers spend more time with their children and are consequently more aware of the extent of their children's handicaps. Mothers also tend to bear more of the burden of their children's daily care, a burden that no doubt promotes a realistic rather than idealistic assessment of their situation. The frequency and intensity of mother-child interaction is also likely to increase the mother's commitment to her role, however, resulting in greater love or acceptance of the child. This interpretation is supported by the interview data to be presented shortly.

The finding that mothers make more consensual statements about their children than fathers do reverses the usual expectation that females will demonstrate a greater socioemotional or expressive orientation while males will think in instrumental terms. This reversal was even more striking in the token "control group," where mothers made almost twice as many consensual statements as fathers did. Perhaps mothers are more likely than fathers to think in consensual terms because they are likely to receive more feedback (consensus) about their children in their everyday interactions. Thus, traditional, stereotyped sex-role distinctions do not seem to apply in this case. This finding suggests a need for further research on the situational nature of sex-role-related perspectives in a normal sample.

In summary, then, the TST results show that these parents of handicapped children tend to define their offspring realistically. Although they wish their children were normal, they are able to appreciate the positive attributes that their children do possess in spite of their handicaps. Mothers tend to be slightly more realistic than fathers, and parents of both sexes are less satisfied with their expectations for the future than with their conceptions of the present. The realistic acceptance that emerges from these data is not necessarily characteristic of *all* parents of congenitally handicapped children. By chance, all of the parents in the study were coping more or less successfully with their situation. Realistic acceptance may, in fact, provide a necessary basis for coping successfully. The processes through which acceptance and coping emerge are explored more fully in the next chapter.

Chapter 5

CAREER DEVELOPMENT: FROM ANOMIE TO ACTIVISM

The Career Path

Because the parent interview generally proceeded in chronological order, beginning with the prenatal period, the resulting data will be presented using the same time sequence as a guide. The following chapter, then, will trace some typical career paths in terms of interactional sequences and resulting patterns of parental response from the prenatal period to the present. After the general patterns have been traced, several ideal-typical emergent roles will be presented along with some complete cases of families that exemplify those role types. All of the interview data was highly consistent with the TST responses as well as with information found in the case records for each family held by the genetic counseling service from which the sample was drawn.

THE PRENATAL PERIOD

All of the parents in the sample said that they had always wanted to have children, and most of the births in question were planned. For most parents, having children was seen as a normal part of marriage, something they had been socialized to want and expect. Only a few mentioned additional motives, such as wanting a son to carry on the family name or having a need to be needed. One father said that his family had reached its present size (three children) because he was "going along with my wife," who had always wanted a large family. These statements would probably be typical of any group of parents with similar backgrounds, whether their children were normal or handicapped.

Some of the parents had a considerable amount of experience with children before their own were born, while others had little or none. Most had helped care for younger siblings or had been involved with nieces and nephews or the children of friends. Some had babysitting experience, and a few mothers had worked with children professionally as teachers, social workers, or nurses.

On the other hand, most parents had little or no experience with handicapped children. A few did have close friends, neighbors, or relatives whose children were defective, and one man had a father who was physically handicapped. Most people knew *of* someone who was disabled in their family or neighborhood while they were growing up, but in most cases, the relationship was not a close personal one:

> It's amazing how little contact I had with children with problems. (M)[1]

> My sister-in-law had a friend with a handicapped child. I remember my sister-in-law always referred to her as "the cripple." (M)

> I knew kids with physical defects, none of them serious, but I had been through nursing and seen all kinds of defects. (M)

> We got a Christmas card every year from a family with a Down's Syndrome child. They always sent a picture of him along with their other kids. (M)

There was a boy who had polio in my Scout troop. (F)[2]

It was something that didn't affect me personally. (F)

I had a good friend whose father was the founder of a school for the retarded and I saw the kids there. It made me feel sad. (F)

In recalling their reactions to the handicapped before their own children were born, most parent echoed the stigmatizing attitudes and pretense awareness found in other members of society:

I remember the slang terminology you heard on the street: these people were "mental." There were retarded adults in the town, and they were ridiculed. (F)

There were two retarded girls where I grew up. I was scared of them. (M)

I always felt bad when I saw anyone who was handicapped. (M)

You don't want to catch yourself staring. (F)

I knew a severely handicapped girl and all I can remember is feeling very sorry for her. (M)

I didn't want to be exposed to that situation (face-to-face interaction with the handicapped). (F)

I still feel uncomfortable with the handicapped. (F)

Not only had most parents had very little direct experience with the handicapped — most did not have much factual knowledge about various handicaps and birth defects either. Many were *not even aware of the existence* of their child's defect prior to the child's birth. Most were vaguely aware of terms such as mental retardation but had no idea of specific syndromes or manifestations. In most cases, parents held stereotyped, and highly negative, notions about these conditions before their children were born. Because these preexisting definitions serve as the bases on which definitional careers are built, the recalled defintions of a large number of representative respondents are presented below:

> I worked in a nursing home, and there were some older Downs' there. I just knew it was retardation, that's all. (M)
>
> I never heard of Down's...Mental retardation wasn't something you talked about in the house...There wasn't much exposure. (F)
>
> I'd heard the term (Mongoloid), but that's all. (F)
>
> I knew it was a chromosome defect. (M)
>
> We have a friend with a Down's daughter and we've seen her do a lot. (F)
>
> I've heard "Mongoloid" — something I had read in passing in a book or something. Just a freak of nature. (M)
>
> I had heard about _____ Syndrome maybe six months or a year before we heard that Jimmy[3] had it, and it was in an article about Abraham Lincoln, and after I read the article...I thought, "It's a good thing he was shot." So when they told me Jimmy had _____, all I could think was "My God, he should be shot." (Laughter, then serious) You know, it was devastating, really. (M)
>
> I was always afraid to have a child with a birth defect. (M)
>
> I saw adults (with Down's Syndrome) when I was in training. They were on the bad side, so when I had Karen, it was quite a trauma. I didn't realize there were different degrees. (M)
>
> I had never heard of it. (F)
>
> I remember thinking, before I got married, it would be the worst thing that could ever happen to me. (M)
>
> I knew nothing about mental retardation — just the vague stories one hears when growing up. These were "people to be shunned." I was ignorant of any factual knowledge. (F)
>
> I can remember reading books as a child about Dale Evans— I guess she had a Down's Syndrome child.... I thought it was a much more devastating condition than it turns out to be. We didn't really have exposure to children who were different. They were institutionalized. (M)

I had a picture in my mind of a Mongoloid person. (M)

I think I was afraid of it. (M)

I'd heard of it from a book. It was just a terrible picture on a certain page of an abnormal psych book that I can still sort of picture. (M)

We were naive. We didn't know anything about it. When Jeff was born, our older children said, "Didn't you know there's a big risk in having children at your age?" But we really didn't. (F)

Most parents recalled relatively uneventful pregnancies. Although a few were at turning points in their lives, having recently lost a close relative, moved, or changed jobs, most were not. The majority also reported that various significant others at the time were highly supportive with respect to the pregnancy and anticipated birth. A few noted that relatives or acquaintances thought they had too many children already, but these were a very small minority. In general, the experiences of these respondents during this time period were probably not significantly different from those of others in the population with similar backgrounds.

The majority of the parents, especially those who had already had a normal child, did not suspect during the pregnancy period that their child would be defective. Many said, "You see these things, but you think, 'This will never happen to me'." A few, however, did recall strong doubts about the health of their child during the prenatal period:

I always said if it wasn't a girl (respondent already had two normal boys), there was something wrong. It just felt different from my other pregnancies, and my sister-in-law had just lost a baby at seven months. (M)

It was our first child, and I just constantly kept thinking there was something wrong. I don't know why. I was just scared or something. (M)

We just hoped everything would be all right because we had lost one chld, but we didn't *really* think anything would be wrong. (M)

I was worried because I had been dieting, and cyclamates had just been taken off the market. (M)

Sure I worried. It's a natural feeling. You always wonder during the whole nine months, "Will this child be all right?"...mental retardation was the thing that concerned me the most I guess. (M)

I felt very strongly that she was deformed. ...It was a gut feeling...I never was told by a doctor. I just had this feeling that something was the matter. ...She didn't kick as much as I thought she should. (Interviewer: Did you mention your concern to your family?) They all thought I was crazy.... Everyone was just saying, "It's her fear of being pregnant. All pregnant women have this fear." But mine was more than normal. I was really afraid. (This mother had had a difficult pregnancy, marked by various physical complications.) (M)

I thought something might be wrong because I was sick all the time and I wasn't sick at all during my first pregnancy. (M)

All of the respondents just quoted were mothers, and their fears were usually discounted by their significant others on the basis of sex-role stereotyping. If one examines the quotes, however, one can find bases in past experience for most mothers' fears: They had lost a child or had a close relative who lost a child previously, or their pregnancy did not fit with their expectations about how one feels when pregnant. Fathers were perhaps less fearful because their sex-role tends to remove them from everyday concern with pregnancy and child rearing.

Possibly, recall of fears during pregnancy may be heightened among mothers who have given birth to a defective child (and who can now say, "I told you so.") and forgotten or minimized by mothers whose children were normal. The responses of the token "control group" become interesting in

this light. The 10 parents of normal children who were interviewed in fact expressed *greater* concern about birth defects
during their (or their wives') pregnancies than the parents of
the handicapped. The following quotes are illustrative:

I had two miscarriages before I became pregnant with Ricky.
I thought maybe I had bad genes or something. ...It was in
the back of my mind through the whole pregnancy. (M)

Oh, yes! You know you forget these things so fast. ...I worried about the viruses, you know, all the things that toddlers
come down with, I always wondered if I would get it. My
daughter had walking pneumonia, and that worried me.
...Yeah, now I remember. You know, you put all that out of
your mind after you've delivered a healthy baby. (M)

My sister had a child who died of cystic fibrosis, and it was a
very sad experience for the whole family. ...The chances
were very slight, but there was some concern that it could
happen to us. ...I've always been worried about having a
child who was handicapped—one of our friends has a terribly
retarded child—terribly retarded. We were concerned. We
just wanted a healthy child. (F)

We had a very healthy child the first time and here we were
"going to bat" again, so to speak. I was aware of the chance
that this time we might "strike out." (F)

The high degree of concern among these parents may have
occurred as a result of their high educational level: All were
college educated, and most had advanced degrees, including
two in medicine. These mothers and fathers were thus highly
aware of the possibility of various birth defects. In any case,
recall of concern during pregnancy does not seem to be confined to parents of defective children.

In summary, then, the parents of handicapped children in
this study had what are probably relatively typical experiences and expectations prior to their children's births.
Most had planned their pregnancies and were looking for-

ward to birth with happy anticipation. They generally had supportive friends and relatives, and while some were in the midst of turning points in their lives, most were not. Most of the parents had only limited knowledge about birth defects and held stereotyped attitudes toward the handicapped typical of others in society. With a few notable exceptions, these parents were generally not overly concerned during pregnancy with the possibility that their child might be defective.

THE TURNING POINT OF BIRTH OR FIRST INFORMATION AND THE POSTPARTUM PERIOD: AN ANOMIC PHASE

Because most of the parents interviewed had anticipated a normal newborn, they were generally quite surprised and concerned when they learned that their expectations had not been fulfilled. The way in which parents first learn that something is wrong with their child is quite variable. Mothers awake during delivery are usually immediately aware of a very obvious problem such as spina bifida. Less obvious problems such as Down's Syndrome are generally made known to parents within a day or two after birth, and some forms of cerebral palsy or defects such as congenital blindness are sometimes not detected (or more commonly, not revealed to parents) until a baby is several months old. Regardless of the timing of the disclosure, the situation of first information is always a turning point for parents, and almost all of the parents interviewed felt that the situation was not handled in an optimum way by physicians and other medical personnel.

In almost every case, the truth was withheld from parents at first. However, various clues generally indicated that something was not right, and most parents found themselves in a state of suspicion awareness (Glaser and Strauss, 1964) for varying lengths of time. The situation described by the following mother of a Down's Syndrome baby was typical:

I remember very vividly. The doctor did not say anything at all when the baby was born. Then he said, "It's a boy," and the way he hesitated, I immediately said, "Is he all right?" And he said, "He has ten fingers and ten toes," so in the back of my mind I knew there was something wrong. ...(In the morning) he didn't come up with the other babies, and I kept saying, "Where's my baby?" When I think back on it, everyone was hush-hush, saying "There's nothing wrong, he'll be up."

Usually in the case of a defect such as Down's Syndrome, parents are informed within a day or two after the child's birth. Sometimes, however, the period of suspicion awareness may be more protracted:

He was born on Tuesday, and by Thursday, I was suspicious. Nurses would come in and ask to see pictures of my first child; then they would leave quickly. ...The baby wasn't eating well, and once when a nurse came in after a feeding, I told her I was worried. She said, "It's all due to his condition." I asked, "What condition?" but she just walked out. ...Then, the doctor asked me when I was going home. When I said, "Tomorrow," he said, "Good that will give us more time to observe the baby." ...The obstetricians kept asking if I noticed any difference between Joey and my first baby. I said he was weak and not eating. They told me that tests were being done to see why he wasn't eating and that they thought he might have a digestive problem. ...I asked to see the house pediatrician. ...Then my husband arrived to take me home and he said to the doctor, "She doesn't know yet. I'll tell her later." (He had just been told himself.) We took the baby to the car, and on the way home my husband told me. (M)

Sometimes, the clues were even more blunt, as the mother of a spina bifida child recalled,

> When the baby was born, they said, "Oh my God, put her out." That's the first thing they said, "Oh my God, put her out." . . . and the next thing I remember was waking up in the recovery room. . . I had my priest on my left hand and my pediatrician on my right hand. . . and they were trying to get me to sign a piece of paper. . . . I just couldn't believe that this was happening to me and I said to my priest, "Father, what's the matter?" and he said, "You have to sign this release. Your daughter is very sick." And I said to the pediatrician, "What's the matter with her?," and he said, "Don't worry honey, she'll be dead before morning." . . . He said she had something that was too much to talk about, that I shouldn't worry myself. . . . It was a very traumatic time. My husband was in Viet Nam. I just couldn't accept it. . . . Nobody was telling me what this was. . . I was very depressed.

This mother did not learn the true nature of her child's condition until amost two weeks later when she was released from the hospital.

In a few cases, although hospital personnel did not issue any clues, parents still suspected problems from the appearance or size of the baby:

> He only weighed seven and a half pounds and he was over-due. All my other babies were much larger. (M)

> When we held him outside the delivery room, my husband noticed, and I noticed, but we never said it to each other, that his ears were very small. (M)

In cases such as these, parents were often likely to rationalize, or try to make sense of the noticed anomaly by defining it in normal terms. Commonly, they would attribute unusual features to familial inheritance: "She had a high forehead, but my husband has a high forehead too." Such rationalizing techniques were sometimes also used by parents even *after* a diagnosis had been issued by a physician:

My pediatrician came in and told me he thought the baby was
retarded because she had slanted eyes and short fingers. I
wondered how he could tell. . . . Visitors came in and they all
said the baby looked like me. . . . . and she *did* look just like
me. I thought, "Maybe *I've* been retarded all these years and
didn't know it." . . . It took a long time to accept it. (M)

In general, then, the parents are faced with events or observations that do not fit, in McHugh's terminology, with the
theme of having had a normal baby. In some cases, the theme
is established by having had other (normal) children previously; in others, expectations are based on various forms of an-
ticipatory socialization: having heard about the birth experiences of others, having attended childbirth preparation
classes, or having read, heard, or seen about childbirth in the
media. Parents also bring to the childbirth situation their past
interactional experience with respect to the behavior of
medical professionals and self-presentation in general. Rationalization represented one form of trying to make events
congruent with expectations, to create order out of an
anomic situation. Techniques such as rationalization tended
to be short-lived, however, and as dissonant cues ac-
cumulated, most parents became intent on learning the truth.

Most parents felt quite resentful toward doctors and nurses
who denied the truth. Some claimed to have been cynical
about doctors even before their children were born, but
others were quite disillusioned by the childbirth experience:

I asked what was wrong with her ears, and they said not to
worry about it. . . . I always thought they told you the truth in
the hospital and if you wanted to know anything you should
ask. I really thought her ears looked funny and I had this funny feeling, so I asked the doctor, "Is there anything wrong?,"
and he looked right at me and said, "No." So I assumed she
was O.K., and there was nothing wrong with her. . . . The next
morning he told me she was retarded. . . . I was very bitter

about it. I think I had the shortest stay in the hospital that anyone ever had. That afternoon I just picked up and left. . . . Later I asked my obstetrician why he never told me, and he said, "It's up to the pediatrician to tell you." Well, I think he should have told me. I never went back to him. . . .

I had had the same pediatrician for six years, and he had always been truthful. I trusted him. . . . I guess he felt that I didn't need to know at that time. . . .

My husband had just called everyone and told them we had a healthy baby and for 24 hours that's all he knew. Now he had to call them all back and tell them there was something wrong. (M)

In another case, the mother was a nurse. Consequently, when the delivery room nurses did not tell her what was wrong with her baby, she defined the situation very differently:

As a nurse, I couldn't tell mothers about their children's defects if they hadn't been told by the doctor yet. You kind of had to lie all the time. . . .

When Billy was born I heard the nurse say, "Is it a boy or a girl?" and I knew right away something was wrong. . . . They wrapped him up so I could just see his head and they said, "We're going to bring him to the nursery now." I let him go because I knew something was wrong and I wanted him to be taken to where he would get attention.

Although many physicians were described as being reluctant to tell the truth, some were reported to be more straightforward, particularly in the case of obvious *physical* defects. Even when doctors were truthful, however, parents often complained about the manner in which the truth was told. Many felt that the physicians in these cases still tended to be evasive, that even though they diagnosed some named defect, they did not explain in detail what the defect *meant*, that is, how it would affect the lives of the child and the family:

> The doctor came in and said "Her cheekbones are high and her eyes...it could be her German ancestry." You know, he hemmed and hawed. I thought she was blind or something. He finally said it was Down's Syndrome. ...We didn't know what it was. My husband looked it up in the encyclopedia. (M)

> They were very evasive, didn't want to talk about it. And then I found a bunch of medical students up at the nurses' station looking at this book of naked people with _____ Syndrome — who looked amazingly like my son, although they tried very hard to hide the book. (M)

> (In the recovery room) the head of pediatrics asked where my husband was. I said I didn't know, and he said, "Maybe I should come back." I said, "What's the problem?" because I immediately sensed there was a problem. He said, "No, I'll wait and talk to you later." I said, "You might as well discuss it with me now." ...He said, "Well, there's a problem, and it's serious, but as an alternative, the child could be institutionalized." — and that's how Danny's birth was first explained. ...I didn't want to see him; I thought it was so bad. (The child had Down's Syndrome.)

Quite a few of the parents felt, as the mother just quoted, that in addition to being evasive, doctors tended to be overly negative in their description of the child's condition:

> The doctor called me and said that there was a question about the baby's health, that there was concern over whether we had a "good baby," that some doctors seem to think he's Mongoloid. (F)

> The pediatrician said, "You baby has _____ Syndrome. Here's some information you can read about it, but don't worry, she probably won't live." (M)

> The doctor said, "In a year you should make an application for training school. Then, at 3 or 4, she'll be institutionalized." (Father of a Down's Syndrome child.)
>
> I knew there was something wrong with the baby. Nobody said a word. I asked the doctor, "What's wrong with the baby?," and he said, "Nothing's wrong with the baby." So I left it at that. I went home and told all my friends we had a healthy baby. . . . (Later) I went back to the hospital, and the doctor told me. *He approached it like it was a disaster*. He said she was Mongoloid, and I asked him how he knew. He said there were traits. I said, "What traits?" and he wouldn't tell me. He said, "I don't want you gaping at the baby." "She's my baby, and I want to know what the traits are." (F)

Another common complaint about the situation of first information was that physicians often told only one parent about a baby's problem without making any attempt to contact the other parent. Although the father was sometimes informed first, more commonly, the unsuspecting father would come to visit his wife in the hospital and find her upset over having just received the bad news. The following experience of a mother who had just been told her baby would probably not live is typical:

> I started crying, and I'm not the type that cries. . . . Then (my husband) walked in with my girlfriend, who's a nurse at _____ Hospital, with the stuffed animals and the flowers and the chocolates. He had gone home thinking that it was only a minor problem and everything would be corrected by surgery.

Most of these fathers complained bitterly that the doctor should have stayed a few more minutes and told both parents together. As one father said, "This was probably the most important thing he would ever say to us."

Although most respondents were critical of the manner in which they were informed about their children's problems, a small minority praised their physicians for being direct and truthful. A few said they were afraid to hear the truth at first, but the desire for information quickly overpowered their fear and they, like the others, were soon asking questions in an attempt to learn the truth. All of the respondents, then, seemed to feel that at the beginning, their greatest need was for information.

A second need, and one that generally arose immediately after some verison of the truth was secured, was for emotional support. Here again, doctors and hospital personnel were felt to be lacking. Many mothers felt that the nurses ignored them in the hospital in favor of mothers with healthy newborns. Those who were not in private rooms were also upset by all of the normal baby activity around them.

For all of these parents, the immediate postpartum period was not a happy time. Both mothers and fathers recalled feelings of self-pity and concerns about the future. The following responses are representative:

I was only (in the hospital) a day. I didn't like the idea of sitting there looking at the four walls feeling sorry for myself. (M)

I was worried they could somehow take her away from me and put her in an institution. (M)

I was thinking of all the retarded people I'd seen. I wasn't thinking about my little girl anymore. (M)

We both cried. What were we going to tell people? (M)

I felt sick. I kept thinking, "I never should have had him." (M)

I was kind of turned off. I didn't want to go near her. It was like she had a disease or something and I didn't want to catch it. I didn't want to touch her. . . . I felt sorry for her. I felt she got gypped out of everything in life. (M)

I sat on the floor crying, never even thinking about (the baby), who she was or where she was. (F)

I saw her for the first time when she was 10 days old. ...I think I was the most petrified I'd ever been in my life, turning that corner and wondering what I would see. ...She was much more deformed than I had been told. At the time, I thought, "Oh my God, what have I done?" (M)

I called (my mother-in-law). Just saying it to her was very difficult at that point. (F)

In most cases, the period of acute self-pity was short-lived as a result of supportive interaction with family, friends, and also with the child:

I talked to a nurse and then I felt less resentment. I said I was afraid, and she helped me feed the baby. ...Then my girlfriend came to see me. She had just lost her husband, and we sort of supported each other. ...By the time she came home I loved her. When I held her the first time I felt love and I worried if she'd live. (M)

As times goes on, you fall in love. You think, "This kid's mine and nobody's gonna take her away from me." I think by the time she was 2 weeks old I wasn't appalled by her anymore. (M)

Everybody was saying he was so lucky to have *us* as parents. (F) (After first deciding not to send out birth announcements, this father reconsidered and printed his own announcements in the form of theater tickets for a hypothetical play entitled, "A Very Special Person.")

Thus, the guilt and self-pity phase, on which so many writers dwell, seems to be real but hardly permanent in these cases. Given the very negative attitudes toward handicapped children that these parents held prenatally, feelings of grief are certainly understandable. However, parents are also socialized to love their children, and the parents in this study seem to have come to that love and acceptance fairly quickly. Convincing the rest of the world that their child was worth loving was considerably more difficult for most parents, and their efforts in this regard will be discussed in detail in a later section.

In some cases, although a defect had been diagnosed at birth, its seriousness did not become apparent to parents until a later time. The phase of shock and grief was delayed for these parents, because the situaton, once defined, had to be redefined and reinterpreted. Such a turning point sometimes occurred when parents first brought their child to a medical specialist. One mother, who believed that her child's problems were largely physical and amenable to surgical correction, discovered to her dismay that her child might be retarded as well:

> Dr. Smith was the first one to really go into detail about (the syndrome). What really got me upset was the book with those really ugly pictures and the fact that I saw "Mental Retardation" on the cover. . . . He asked me, "What do you think of mental retardation?" When I think of mental retardation I think of a kid that is real bad, you know. . . . I wasn't ready for it. . . . . When I came home I cried all afternoon.

In other cases, developmental problems became apparent slowly in children whose physical defects were obvious at birth. Sometimes, problems seemed to reveal themselves in stages, as in the case of one child who, at birth, had deformed hands and feet. The parents were told to wait and see if other problems developed but they did not realize that these might be serious. Later, heart problems became apparent, and eventually, mental retardation was evident. In another case, the parents felt that doctors were aware of many problems that they chose to reveal to the parents only gradually, creating severe definitional problems:

> Every time we went, they told us something else. It's my feeling that you can't really cope unless you know the whole

truth. ...You can't cope in stages. ...I kept expecting something else. (M)

The anomic period is thus protracted in such cases, and acceptance is delayed.

A definitional crisis also arises in the case of parents whose child, defined at birth as perfectly normal and healthy, is later diagnosed as defective. The shock and disbelief are likely to be greater in such cases than in those of early diagnosis. Sometimes, however, this situation is only a protraction of the one already discussed, in which physicians delay in revealing the truth to parents who are already suspicious as a result of various clues.

Sometimes, clues are present, but are defined within a framework of normality by parents, especially when this framework is supported by significant others, including physicians. In one very unusual case in the sample, a defect was not diagnosed until the child was 12 years old. As the child's mother explained,

When he was 2, all of a sudden his face seemed extremely long....In third grade, I had to make all his pants. That's when it became obvious that this kid is not made like other kids because you can't buy any clothes to fit him. ...But I just thought he was a tall skinny kid. ...He had had regular checkups. ...He was doing well in school. ...We knew he ran funny. He walked late and was seen at _____Children's Hospital, but they didn't see anything unusual....Then, when he was 12 years old, the doctor found a heart murmur, and he was admitted to the hospital (where his defect was diagnosed).

In three cases of relatively late diagnosis (at ages two months, six months and eight months), clues were either not apparent to parents or were defined as unimportant by them. In one instance, during a routine visit to the pediatrician, the mother thought she saw something in the baby's eye and asked the nurse to check. After the nurse looked at the baby, her tone became grave, and she rushed to get the doctor, who told the parents that their child had cataracts and was blind. In another case, the parents had Christmas pictures taken of their daughter and noticed that, in the pictures, "her eye was like shining back at you." They were not concerned enough to call the doctor at the time, but the mother mentioned it to the pediatrician at the next routine checkup and was told that a tumor was present and the eye would probably have to be removed. In both of these cases, the parents were naturally very shocked by the diagnosis.

In a similar situation, the parents were aware that their baby had some problems but they had attributed these to the fact that she was premature. The child was a twin, whose sister was stillborn. After the birth, the parents were told, "The other baby's fine," and the mother "didn't realize that anything could still go wrong." The baby was hard to feed, but the mother "thought it was just because she was a premie." When the baby was 6 months old, the mother began to realize that her daughter "was not holding things like other babies" but again attributed the slowness to her prematurity. When, at the baby's regular 6-month checkup, the pediatrician suggested the possibility of cerebral palsy, the mother "just broke down completely in his office." She said that she "just couldn't believe it." This mother called her husband from the doctor's office, and his recollection of the situation follows:

> It was out of the blue. . . .(My wife) called me up at work and said that Dr. _____ thought Kathy might have cerebral palsy, and that was the first time that ever entered my mind. . . .She was our first child, and I had no knowledge of what was normal and what was abnormal.

Such a situation was less likely to arise when the defective child had older siblings. In three other cases of relatively late diagnosis, experienced parents insisted to their physicians that problems existed even though their doctors denied their existence. In one such case, the mother suspected from the beginning that something might be wrong with her baby:

> She wouldn't nurse in the hospital. ...Then her eyes were crossing, and she always seemed to be looking at her right side. ...I questioned her vision and hearing, but the doctor said there was nothing wrong. ...When she was 3 months old, we had her picture taken, and she kept falling alseep. I think the photographer knew there was something wrong, because they take pictures of so many children. ...Then, when she was 5 months old, it was really obvious that there was something wrong. She had seizures or something. There were periods when she would come and go.

This mother had an older child and also had a sister who had a baby 10 days older than hers and a neighbor whose baby was a week younger. She was also a nurse. As a result, she was very aware of her baby's differentness. Because her pediatrician insisted that nothing was wrong with the child, she began blaming herself: "I thought, well maybe I'm not giving her enough time. I had this older child...who was not too happy about having a sister (and I spent most of my time with him)." Finally, when the baby was 6 months old, the mother "broke down and started crying" in the doctor's office, insisting that something was wrong, and the doctor initiated diagnostic tests. The child was finally diagnosed as retarded when she was about a year old. At that point, the mother was more relieved than shocked by the diagnosis.

In a similar case, the mother was worried from the beginning because her son would not eat:

> They kept saying, "Oh, he's little, he'll pick up." It should have been obvious to the doctors and nurses that there was something wrong with the way he was sucking. ...His prob-

lem was the cerebral palsy, the hypotonia. He just didn't have the muscle control in his mouth and neck — to suck. And that was his problem. He was literally starving to death. (Interviewer: Did you ask your pediatrician about it?) I asked everyone. When I left the hospital, I was saying, "He's not eating, he's not eating." But they probably hear this from 90% of the mothers.

When this mother got home from the hospital, the baby was "crying all the time." She called her pediatrician, and he told her that the baby probably had colic and prescribed a sedative. Finally, "the baby stopped crying altogether. He never even woke up for his feedings." When the frantic mother brought the baby to the pediatrician for his first checkup at 6 weeks, the child was immediately hospitalized for "failure to thrive," and his cerebral palsy was eventually diagnosed. Both this case and the preceding one are reminiscent of a case reported by Hewett (see quote on bottom of page 58).

Although both the mothers just discussed were very concerned about their children, they were perhaps not more insistent with their doctors for two reasons. First of all, they were reluctant to challenge the physician's professional dominance, and secondly, their significant others were not entirely supportive of the fact that a problem existed. The second mother noted that *after* her son's problem was diagnosed, her mother said, "I *thought* something was wrong." However, while this mother was struggling to feed the infant, her mother and others had reassured her and rationalized the problem. The husbands in both cases were also apparently unconcerned at first. As the first one explained,

(My wife) was very concerned because the baby was...not sucking. It grew into something bigger and bigger as the months went by. ...I thought she was a little paranoid about it. When she got very upset, I began to realize that maybe there *was* something wrong. When you're not home all day you don't

see the (baby's) lack of activity or anything like that. Maybe I
was being like an ostrich. I pretty much ignored everything.
...I was very little wrapped up in it.

In such an interaction situation, a mother is likely to feel a
great deal of concern, conflict, and self-doubt, and both of
these mothers described themselves as being "on the verge of
a breakdown" during this anomic period in their lives.

In the only other instance of delayed diagnosis in the sample, the syndrome involved had an apparently sudden onset
after the baby seemed normal for the first few months of life.
This case is particularly interesting because it involved four
children in the same family and a different situation of
redefinition each time.

The first of the affected children in the family had an
older, normal sibling, and for the first eight months of his
life, his parents defined him as bright because he seemed to be
developing much more quickly than his older brother. His
mother describes the change:

> He started to cry one day. ...I called the pediatrician and
> said, "He's crying night and day and he won't even hold his
> head up." He said, "He's probably teething."
> Finally, we came to see him. He said it was tonsilitis and
> gave him antibiotics. He said he'd be all right in a few days.
> Tony still wouldn't hold his head up. ...The pediatrician
> said, "We'll give him some tonic to build him up." Well, we
> gave him one bottle of tonic, two bottles of tonic, and he still
> wouldn't hold his head up. We started getting very worried. I
> became very aware of the TV campaigns for different kinds
> of handicaps and I'd listen very carefully to the symptoms
> and think, "Oh my God he has this; does he have that?"
> Then Tony got worse and worse. His legs tightened up and
> scissored in. We finally put him in _____ Hospital for obser-
> vation. We thought he was going to die.

By the time this child's diagnosis was established, the

mother was already pregnant with her third child. When she asked her doctor whether her unborn child could have the same problem, she remembers being told, "Don't even think about it. This happens once in every...for God sakes don't even think about it." She describes the onset of her third child's problem as follows:

> At birth she looked good. ...When she was 6 months old she caught chicken pox from my brother's children and she was never the same. ...They told us at the hospital, "She's probably blind and retarded, maybe deaf too, but it's not cerebral palsy."

The family later learned that their daughter's problem *was* the same cerebral palsy-like syndrome that affected their son.

Three years later, this mother found herself pregnant again. Once more she was told that the problem was not likely to recur. She says, "I was unrealistic. I said, 'He's going to be a Christmas baby. There won't be anything wrong with him'." This fourth baby was watched very carefully from birth, and at his 6-month checkup, his mother recalls that the doctor said,

> "Mrs. Jones, you've made it. You don't have to worry, the baby is perfectly normal." ...We were just so happy. ...Two weeks later, Richie started to cry and he didn't want to hold his head up. (I called the doctor, and he said), "We just went over him, and he looked fine. You know he's teething." ...We started the iron tonic again. ...Then we insisted he go into the hospital.

After a diagnosis was made, this mother was told by the hospital staff that her pediatrician "had suspected it all along," whereupon she became furious:

> Well if I had a gun I would have shot him. I thought that was so unprofessional. Here I had been telling them how well he

was doing. ... "Look," I said, "This is our third child with this. I don't want to hide anything. I want to know why this is happening."

She showed the hospital staff pictures of this child, taken just several weeks earlier, in which he was swinging in a swing and performing normal motor activities. The staff doctor said he believed her. As a result of this incident, she never went back to her former pediatrician.

When this mother found herself pregnant for the fifth time three years later, her new pediatrician advised her to have an abortion. The mother refused, and again, her newborn child was watched very closely by doctors. At five months,

> the baby's hand started to turn in. I said, "Oh my God not again, not all over." I couldn't believe it. ... You just don't have that many handicapped kids. ... When I found out Nancy was like this too, I was just numb. I had no feelings.

One might be tempted to attribute these negative recollections of birth and postpartum experiences to defensive projection by parents of defective children. However, in the small check sample of parents of normal children, quite a few complaints about the performance of medical professionals in the birth situation were also present. Perhaps preconceived notions about the nature of the birth situation are only sometimes fulfilled.

In general then, the situation of first being informed of a child's birth defect, is a highly negative turning point for parents. Even those parents who suspected prenatally that their baby might be defective, were very upset to learn that their suspicions had been confirmed. Because most parents have very limited knowledge of birth defects prenatally, the situation of first information tends at first to be an anomic one. When their child is labeled for the first time, parents are likely to ask, "What does it mean?" The postpartum period, then, eventually gives way to a phase of seekership (Lofland and Stark, 1965), in which parents begin to search for realistic definitions and solutions.

THE SEEKERSHIP PHASE: INFANCY AND BEYOND

Almost all of the parents in the sample felt that at the beginning their greatest need was for information. Even those who were told the exact nature of their child's condition immediately said that they were left with an empty feeling of not knowing what to do. When a normal child is born, relatives, friends, and neighbors abound with advice for the new parents. The respondents here generally had a different experience — they felt alone.

In a few cases, significant others, especially the child's grandparents, were not very helpful because they continued to deny the seriousness of the child's condition even after the parents had accepted it:

(My mother-in-law said), "She's only five days old and she's turned over already. How can she be retarded?" (M)

Up until this day, my parents don't want to accept that she's handicapped and retarded. (Child is 5 years old) (F)

My parents kept saying, "You had hair like that when you were born." (F)

The neighbors all said, "Oh, there's nothing wrong with him. He looks fine." ...My sister-in-law keeps saying, "He's doing everything he should be doing." (This father of a Down's Syndrome infant was the only parent in the sample who was not completely convinced at the time of the interview that his child had been diagnosed correctly.)

(My in-laws) to this day will not accept her as retarded. They will not say the word. They don't like us to talk about retardation. ...She's their only grandchild. (M)

My wife's mother still thinks that Billy's going to do something someday, that he will be cured. (F)

My mother thought that if she prayed hard enough, Susan would be O.K. My father would accept that Susan was small but he would never accept that she would be retarded. (M)

My mother loves Debbie and is proud of her but she doesn't admit how really dreadful Debbie's vision is. (M)

In a few other cases, parents felt alone because they declined, for various reasons, to tell friends and relatives about their child's problem. Some said they were not ashamed but "just didn't want to explain." In one case, the wife's sister was expecting a baby at the time, and the couple did not want to upset her. This mother described the four months of secrecy until her sister's baby was born as "terrible." After the family in this case was told, several members remarked that they had "realized it all along" anyway.

None of the parents kept their child's condition secret for very long. As one couple remarked, "After a week we told people. We realized that we were going to have to live with it." Almost all reported that their families and friends were sympathetic and supportive when they were first told:

The thing that surprised me was that everyone accepted it rigth off. (M)

People were extra nice to me. (M)

My boss was understanding because he has a child with a birth defect. (F)

My twin sister checked on the baby for me every day I was in the hospital. (M)

I called my mother as soon as I knew, and she came over. She was very supportive. (M)

My father said, "What's the difference? She's yours." (F)

Although friends and relatives were generally sympathetic and accepting, they were not very helpful in providing concrete information about raising a handicapped child. Thus, most parents had to search elsewhere for answers to their questions. Some had been given perfunctory advice by pediatricians but felt that being told, "Treat the baby like a normal child" was not sufficient, especially when the child did not respond "normally" to parental efforts. The parental seekership that ensued took various forms:

I called my pediatrician but he didn't know anything about _____ Syndrome. I called a friend who was a doctor, and he didn't know much either. (M)

The doctor sent us to the _____ Child Study Center. . . . We went there for two and a half years, but they never did anything there. So I called _____ Children's Hospital — I had always heard it was for crippled children — and we were accepted there. My pediatrician said we were foolish to go there. He said, "You know, Mrs. Jones, he'll never be normal." (M)

I went to the library and looked in the encyclopedia. There really wasn't anyplace to find anything. (M)

I looked it up in the dictionary and called the doctor. He said in a year we should make an application for training school, and she would be institutionalized at 3 or 4. I didn't like that answer. (F)

(The medical literature) was absolutely grotesque. I couldn't look at it. We didn't know what we were going to do. . . . (My husband) went to the March of Dimes, but they had no information available. They recommended Dr. Smith. . . . We wanted to get *us* in control instead of everybody else. (M)

(The neurologist said), "I think I know what's wrong with your son but I'm not going to tell you because I don't want to frighten you." Well, I think that's about the worst thing anyone could say. . . . We didn't go back to him. . . . We insisted that our doctor refer us to _____ Children's Hospital, but the doctor said, "He's little. Why don't you wait? You don't need to take him there yet." I have a feeling that he knew what the diagnosis was going to be and he didn't really think that we needed to know yet. . . . everyone was pablum-feeding us, and we wanted the truth. (M)

The eye doctor said they could operate in two years and we should bring her back in six months. We called my brother-in-law, who is a pediatrician. ...He told us to take her to _____ (City), and she had surgery two months later. I was relieved that something could be done sooner than two years. (F)

A neighbor, who had been a nurse, came over. I asked her for information, but she wouldn't show me her nursing books. ...What do you do with a Mongoloid child? I had no idea what was available for help. I was completely at a loss. It was three weeks before we talked with anyone who gave us any information. ...People said he'd do everything a normal child does, but I didn't believe it. He didn't even open his eyes until he was 5 days old. (M)

The whole first year we didn't see anyone or go anywhere. I was worried what she would be like when she grew up. Would she be toilet trained? Would she walk or talk or do things like that? Who would take care of her if anything happened to us?...Our pediatrician kept putting us off, saying "She's still too young." ...I went down to the Visiting Nurse Association just to get some information, a pamphlet, anything, about Mongolism.

Finally, a friend of mine...called and said she thought she saw a girlfriend of ours that we'd gone to school with in the doctor's office, and she said that her daughter said that there was a little girl there that looked like Michelle. I thought about it...I hadn't talked to this girl since we graduated from high school. I called her up and said, "You have a daughter, right?" And she said, "Yes." I said, "I want to ask you a question. I don't want you to feel offended," I said, "if I'm wrong, I'm sorry." I said, "Is your daughter a Mongoloid?" she said, "Yes she is. How did you know?" I explained to her how I found out. She was our first exposure to other retarded people (She told us about different programs and the Association for the Retarded). We had never even realized there was a school for retarded children. (M)

When you're told something like this you can't go and look it up in the encyclopedia. My encyclopedia doesn't even mention it. The encyclopedia at the library mentioned it in a paragraph. Nobody had any information at all. Your questions come, not when you're sitting there with the doctor, but later, when you get home and start to think about it. (M)

I was looking for a door at that point — somebody who could give us any help at all. Dr. _____ didn't even tell us there was a state agency that dealt with mental retardation. (M)

At this stage, then, parents typically find themselves playing the role of researcher, exploring all available resources in their quest for information and guidance. Dr. Spock is simply inadequate for these families, who like others in society, have been socialized to want to raise their children properly. The drive for knowledge and help can become quite overpowering, as these parents seek to eliminate the anomie they feel. As one mother said, "You went to bed thinking _____ Syndrome and you woke up thinking _____ Syndrome. You couldn't do anything else."

In a few cases, the need for information was delayed by an initial prognosis that the child would not live. These parents were generally so obsessed with their child's impending death that information about the child's specific condition seemed relatively unimportant at the time:

The doctor told me, "She's going to turn blue when you feed her." . . . I was running to the phone every time her feet were cold. (M)

The doctor wanted to see my other children. He said, "They're normal. You have nothing to worry about. You have two normal children. Don't worry about this one. He'll probably only live to be 8 months old. Put him in an institution and forget about him." . . . I'm a nurse and I knew what institutions were like. A child like Billy would not have survived even eight months in an institution. So we brought him home. (M)

The whole first year I was afraid she would die but I also hoped she would die. She just cried all the time. I went to bed at night thinking, "May the angels take you, little girl." (M)

He was misdiagnosed as microcephalic by the neurosurgeon who thought he was 6 months old instead of 6 weeks old. We lived with the wrong diagnosis for three weeks. We were told he would only live about a year and if he lived longer he would have to be institutionalized because he would be a psychological problem to (his older sister). That was a ten minute medical pronouncement. . . . Then the baby started smiling, and the doctor had said he wouldn't do *anything*. We asked to see a neurologist, and the first thing he said was, "No, he's not microcephalic." (M)

I find it difficult to discuss the early weeks. Dr. _____ said he wouldn't live 10 days. I thought, "This two weeks of trying to find out about retardation has been wasted." I felt as though my burden had been lifted. The doctor made the baby cry and she said, "My God, he turns black." I thought in a few weeks it would be over. We would take a vacation. Then the doctor said it would be a slow lingering death, and we could put him in the hospital at the end.

Later, when we went back to Dr. _____, his color had improved, and she said, "It will be months." I thought, "Don't let him die over Christmas." We got baby gifts, and I thought, "He'll never wear it." . . . After awhile, I remember saying, "I can't help getting attached to him." (M)

In all of these cases, the prognosis changed, and the parents entered a seekership phase similar to that of the other parents in the study.

Once their need for information has been somewhat satisfied, most parents channel their seekership in other directions. Typical needs that emerge at this point include: (1) obtaining satisfactory medical treatment for the handicapped child, (2) securing social acceptance of the handicapped child, (3) finding appropriate educational or training programs, and (4) securing other services, such as financial aid or competent babysitters.

The most common complaint among these parents was that the medical treatment their children received had often been delivered in a rude and dehumanizing way:

After he was born, he went to _____ Hospital in _____ (City) for two weeks. ...When we picked him up, he had no diapers on (parents had told staff that baby should wear diapers to avoid hip dislocation), a dislocated hip, ...a rash...and he had lost weight. ...He was discharged only with a diagnosis of "congenital defects," and nothing more. (M)

Whenever there's something wrong, our pediatrician says, "I don't know what I can do for you. That's her condition." ...Our pediatrician thinks my daughter's a freak, totally untrainable, completely retarded. ...He says, "She's retarded and there's nothing you can do about it. You're wasting your time going to specialists." He blames all of her (medical) problems on retardation instead of treating them. (M)

My pediatrician kept after me to put him away (in an institution). (We finally changed pediatricians.) Our new pediatrician gushed all over us at first. ...But then, he never touched Billy. I always had to move him for him. We were never left in the waiting room. It was like I was an embarrassment. ...When Billy was in the hospital, our old pediatrician stuck his head in the door and said, "it's too bad he couldn't go (die)." ...The doctors on rounds would talk outside our door and they ripped apart parents who keep their (severely handicapped) children. (M)

Two years ago, Billy got pneumonia, and we took him to the hospital. They said, "Take him home and let him die." I thought, "He's going to die on us, we've got to do something." (The parents then drove 200 miles to take the child to a sympathetic doctor they had known in another city.)...

It's like when you take your dog to the vet. ...Not many doctors pick him up and try to communicate with him as a child. (F)

She has a problem with her knee, and we took her to _____ Children's Hospital. ...They said, "There's nothing we can do with one of *these* children." (Child has Down's Syndrome.) (F)

(Our pediatrician) seemed to feel that Brian was an unnecessary burden and we really shouldn't bother about him. ...He didn't take my complaints seriously. ...I feel that Brian's sore throat is just as important as (my normal daughter's) sore throat. (M)

The pediatrician didn't seem to be interested in anyone with a problem...He would keep him alive but he wasn't interested in Brian as a person. (F)

(Our pediatrician) treated her as an article in a medical journal. (M)

We went to the clinic at _____ Children's Hospital. ...We saw a different doctor every time and we always had to wait a long time. One time, Kathy was so fussy by the time they got around to examining her, they couldn't even examine her. ...The doctors treated her like a "thing." (M)

Doctors' technical competence was questioned less often than their lack of compassion, concern, and understanding of parents' feelings. Because most parents had come to love and accept their children rather early they were generally upset by doctors who saw their children as less than human or who recommended early institutionalization. Consultations with doctors also often constituted important definitional turning points for parents, so that a doctor's attitude was sometimes a source of expecially great concern to parents. The following experience was somewhat typical:

Just going to _____ Children's Hospital was an emotional experience. I had never been exposed to the world of the handicapped. Seeing all those children in wheelchairs and braces made me think of Kathy. ...I got the impression that (the doctor) didn't understand why I was so upset. He kept saying, "Why are you crying?" (M)

Another source of concern to parents, and one that is most common among parents whose children have serious, continuing medical problems, is the realization of professional dominance. After a period of quiet submission, most of these parents began to take steps to regain control over their children's lives and medical treatment:

> The doctor said, "Professionals, not parents, should decide on institutionalization." I didn't like that. (F)

> In all of her hospitalizations I've been very frustrated by residents who think they know everything. They've given us so much misinformation and details we didn't want to hear. ...Now I tell them. ...I find that other parents are too accepting. They don't question their doctors. (M)

> Because nothing was happening, and I was just sitting there with this baby, we got involved with the patterning program.[4] ...It was the first time that anyone had reacted to him as Billy: "Billy is a person and we'll help Billy." We were never told he would be cured. They were the first people who reacted to Billy as a person or called him by name. Up to that time he had done nothing. My pediatrician said, "You're just looking for hopes." I said, "No, I'm just looking to *do* something for him. I'm sitting at home doing nothing." ...Then he started picking his head up for the first time. He opened his eyes. He started crying and reacting to things. (M)

> (When this mother gave birth to a second handicapped child, she reports that her obstetrician said,)

> "You cannot possibly take care of this child. I'll send the social worker up to you, and you can put him away." I was mad at the world and was determined I was going to get through it. My obstetrician got mad at me, and I signed out of the hospital. (This child only lived a few years.)

> Our doctor sent us to _____ Teaching Hospital (about 250 miles away). She was supposed to be a research patient there. We went down twice. The first time they didn't have her admission papers. ...(After the second time), when we finally brought her home, the doctor there said, "Frankly Mrs. Jones, with the hospitals you have in (your state), I don't know why you brought her here." It turned out that she was

just an ordinary admission, not a research patient. . . . We were furious. When we got home, I sent an eight-page letter to the administrator of the hospital. . . . I said I wouldn't pay the (very large) bill. . . . We were broke. Up until that time we had always struggled to pay even though we didn't have the money. We were dumb. We didn't know you could ask for a reduction. (All of the charges at _____ Teaching Hospital were cancelled.) (M)

At the beginning, I let (the doctors) rule me. . . . Now they do like I ask them to. . . . I used to be in awe of them. . . . Now I won't just sign anything. . . . I've complained to nurses. I've changed a lot. . . . We've had a lot of disputes. They would not give her a bottle in the hospital. They thought she was too old to have a bottle at two years. . . .

We were always going back and forth to _____ Children's Hospital. . . . It was a constantly pulling away. We could never be a family. . . . It was always, "We have to go to the hospital." We had to go to doctors, doctors, doctors. . . . We never could get to know our child. . . . We got to the point where we hated doctors, we hated _____ Children's Hospital. (M)

"Undifferentiated mental retardation." What does that mean? What do we do? . . . I felt very strange — hostile — seeing five people watch her put a raisin in a bottle. . . . The diagnosis was not satisfactory, and we didn't know what to do with her. That's when we heard about (the patterning program). (This family later decided against patterning.) (F)

These parents were not looking for miracles or even cures. They were generally reacting against the frustration of continually receiving inappropriate, dehumanizing, and/or incorrect advice from or treatment by medical professionals. Most were seeking a human quality felt to be lacking in their past interactions, and most eventually found that quality. Almost all of the parents reported having eventually found a pediatrician or specialist they liked and respected and who treated their child "like a person." Some did not find such a doctor for a long time, because they were reluctant to leave the unsatisfactory doctor they already had. The constraints of professional dominance are strong in this society and are not easily abandoned. In this situation, a negative turning point often became the straw that broke the camel's back. These parents were then sometimes further encouraged to change physicians after hearing about a successful change made by others in a parents' association. The role of parents' associations in parental careers will be discussed more fully shortly.

A second interactional area in which parental seekership becomes important is that of securing acceptance of the handicapped child, not only by professionals, but by lay persons as well. As noted earlier, most parents did not have *great* difficulty in learning to accept their child at home, because significant others were generally supportive. Convincing *non*-significant others that a child is acceptable is often a more difficult task in a society that has not been structured for close interaction between the handicapped and normals.

Most of the parents reported that they had always taken their child out in public. Many felt uneasy about such excursions at first and engaged in various techniques of impression management to make the child appear normal:

> We took her to a store downtown, and she had a hat. . . . I wanted to make sure that hat would stay tied on so no one would see her ears. . . . Then I said, "We can't go on like this. This is ridiculous." . . . We didn't want people to look at her. We didn't want to explain. . . . I didn't want to talk about it. (M)

> In stores, people say, "Oh, what a beautiful baby!" I want to say, "She's a Down's baby," but I don't. (M)

> The first time I took him out I was nervous that someone would look at him, but everyone who looked at him said how beautiful he was. I didn't tell anyone. (M)

I don't often take her places where there's a lot of school children. Children stare. Kids make fun of her. Sometimes I just stare back. I think maybe I should talk to them. . . . One time. . . (a girl was laughing at her). I wish I had talked to her and asked her, "Why are you laughing?" I could have explained to her. She was about 9 years old. She could understand. . . . I told my family, but they thought I was making it up. They think she's beautiful. . . . I don't want to take her swimming at a public place. Maybe if I had someone to go with me. (M) (This mother is foreign-born and not closely integrated in any friendship networks.)

I'm a perfectionist. When my (normal) son was born, he had a birthmark, and I used to comb his hair down over his forehead to cover it. I won't like having her look "mongoloid." I'm enjoying the fact that it's not obvious now. (M)

(In stores) they look. And I try not to look at them looking. . . . I feel uncomfortable when. . . people come up to her in a grocery store. . . . *I* can't even understand what she's saying. . . . People kind of back off. . . . I usually say, "Come on, Julie, let's go." (F)

I didn't want anyone to see her hands. I kept them hidden under her clothes. (M)

It's becoming a little easier to tell people. It was hard at first. . . . I used to go to the laundromat. . . and so many people would say, "Your little girl is *so* good to sit there so quietly in the stroller. My kids would never do that." I would just like, sit there, and my insides were like knots, and I would think, "Oh no, do I have to tell them about the cerebral palsy? Should I or shouldn't I? Should I just let it pass?. . ." All this is going through my mind. . . . I never told anybody. (M)

It's not on his health record at school. I don't want him to be treated differently. . . . His math teacher said she was concerned because he looked so frail. . . . I said he had a problem but I didn't tell her the whole thing. (M)

Thus, at the beginning, some parents commonly manage impressions by simply *avoiding* stigma-provoking situations. Some parents of infants engaged in *passing*, because their babies did not yet *look* different. As their children get older, and parents feel more secure, most become less reluctant to take their children out in public. Some continue to *pose* in interactions with strangers, however, in order to avoid embarrassment to others. A very common "white lie" in such situations involves "lowering" children's ages to make their chronological ages match their size and/or behavior:

I say, "He's one." (He's actually 18 months old). Then they ask, "Does he walk yet?" I say, "No," (not unusual for a 1 year old). I don't say anything to people in the store, but if I'm going to see someone again, then I do. (M)

He just looked like a little baby, even at 2 or 3. People would ask how old he was — especially waitresses — and then they were embarrassed. So I started lying, and waitresses would say, "Oh, he's so cute!" (M)

When I take him out, I lie about his age if I don't know the people. It's much easier for both of us. (M)

I never knew whether to give his right age, because other people got embarrassed. If it was just someone in a store, I just told them how old he *looked*. (M)

We bought a car last February. Joey was 15 or 16 months old, and the salesman asked, "Is the baby eight or 9 months old?" I said, "Yes." (My daughter) said, "He's one." I said "Sh." I've been a little too hesitant about telling people. (M)

If children *look* their age, the parental conflict is increased:

People ask how old she is. I don't feel like explaining. It's very uncomfortable. I'm not used to it yet. I get very uptight about it. (M)

Generally, after an initial period of avoidance and conflict, parents become more willing to explain their children's problems openly. A few, however, first pass through a phase of sarcasm or hostility to strangers:

> If we're sitting in a restaurant, and somone's gawking at her...then the kids really get down. It upsets them, to the point where they say, "She was born that way. What's your excuse?" I don't stop them from saying that. (F)
>
> I took her everywhere with me, and everyone would ask what was wrong with her. I finally told one woman, "I threw her down a flight of stairs." (M)

Almost all eventually become quite willing to take their children out and to talk about their problem. In fact, several parents noted that explaining to others helped *them* understand their situation better. The following responses reflect the ease with which many parents come to face the public:

> Now it's very obvious that she is retarded...I *hope* they realize she's retarded. I mean, she's six and a half and she's still saying "da-da," "ma-ma." ...I used to be self-conscious about it. We've come a long way over the years. (M)
>
> We take her everywhere. ...(My normal son) said he wanted to have a friend over, and I told him, "No, it's Karen's turn to have a friend over. She doesn't have many friends." And he said, "What do you mean she doesn't have many friends? Everyone in town knows Karen!" (M)
>
> People ask how old he is. When we say "10," they get embarrassed. We explained that he's brain-damaged. (F)
>
> Sometimes, people have thought it was cerebral palsy. If they could label him with something they knew it seemed to make them feel better. So I would explain it by saying, "Yes, it's kind of like cerebral palsy." (M)
>
> People ask how old she is. I tell them and then I tell them, "She's handicapped." ...I take her out. If you stop taking

her places, it gets too easy to leave her home. . . . That would be depriving *her*. (M)

When we moved here, a neighbor had a tea for me. Everyone had their children there, and I brought Kathy. I gave Kathy a drink — she has trouble drinking — and the neighbors said, "Oh, it went down the wrong way." I said, "No, Kathy has cerebral palsy." I thought, "These are going to be my neighbors, I have to tell them." Everybody was really nice about it. (M)

Parental honesty can sometimes create embarrassment for the curious stranger who does not expect to hear that a child has a *serious* problem, as the following case illustrates:

People asked why she wore a patch. They were shocked when I told them she had no eye. . . . Once a lady asked, "Is there something wrong with her eye?" I said, "Yes. It's artificial." Then . . . Laurie took out her eye, and the lady was really horrified. (F)

In other situations, parental candor is sometimes met by reactions that parents find offensive:

People pitied us. Some people would pick one of them up and say, "Now let's see if you can really take a step," and that really killed us. Some of these people were elderly and you didn't want to be cruel to them and yet you wanted to hit them over the head. Then, some people would say, "You'd be better off it they died." This used to hurt too. I said, "They're not bothering you. They're no burden to you." (M)

People think that retardation is a contagious disease. . . . I don't understand how it threatens them . . . the fact that a van pulls up in our driveway, picks up our daughter, and takes her to a program. (F)

They're sorry at first. . . . Then I just keep right on talking like they hadn't even said anything. Then maybe they think, "*She*'s not sorry." (M)

The first thing they say is, "I'm sorry." The next thing they say is, "They're such loving children." I'm so tired of hearing that. The other thing is, everyone seems to know someone who had it in their family. (M)

The neighbors just ignore our kids. Nobody ever offers to help lift a wheelchair. (F)

When I walk down the street with just Susan, people say "Hi" from their yards. When I walk down the street with Susan and Jenny (Susan's normal sister), they come over and relate to Jenny. People don't know how to relate to Susan. (M)

Some children tease her, and it makes me angry, especially when their parents are with them. (F)

When she was little, people were afraid to say anything. They would ask how (her normal brother) was doing, but just asking about Julie was like a personal question. (M)

Thus, while most parents welcome genuine interest in their handicapped children, they do *not* appreciate pseudoconcern in the form of stereotyped expressions of sympathy. They also feel antagonistic toward negative or stigmatizing reactions, such as avoidance.

The negative reactions of others do not affect parents' feelings toward their children, since these others are not significant to parents. If anything, they become an out-group, and their existence increases the cohesion of the in-group of significant others. As Goffman has suggested, the in-group consists of the own and the wise. The own in this case includes parents' associations and other individual parents with handicapped children, while the wise generally includes a small core of supportive family members and occasionally, a friend, neighbor, or professional.

A very large number of parents in the sample reported friendships with other parents of handicapped children. Sometimes, their friends' children had handicaps that were quite different from those of their own children, suggesting that the *societal reaction* is similar for a variety of medical conditions. A mother of a Down's Syndrome child, for example, mentioned that her best friend had a daughter with spina bifida. She said, "I think we became best friends because we both had handicapped children."

Sometimes other parents play a functional role in addition to simply being friends:

> It's the parents that keep you going. . . . You see them in the waiting room during surgery and you feel better knowing someone else has already gone through it. . . . Sometimes, a mother looked after my child (in the hospital) when I wasn't able to visit, and I would look after hers. (M)

Other handicapped children in a neighborhood also sometimes serve as playmates for the defective child, while the parents visit and support each other.

Some parents reported that they tended to be friendlier with other parents of handicapped children when their children were younger and their seekership needs greater. Another function of such acquaintanceships is to help parents see the positive aspects of their own children's conditions:

> I was in a once-a-week mothers' group, and it was very helpful. You find out you're not the only person with this problem. You don't feel sorry for yourself when you see some children that are just vegetables. (M)

> We went to a couples' group where we saw that other children were a lot worse than Peter. (F)

> I have a girlfriend with a boy with muscular dystrophy. Before I knew her I felt, "It just happens to me." (M)

> We went to the Association pretty regularly for two years. But after awhile we felt that they did not have that much to offer...as far as help to us. Karen went to their nursery

school, but we just got too busy to go to the meetings. Karen didn't have a lot of problems. We did become friendly with another family with a Down's child through the Association. We don't get together socially but we're good friends because of the children. (M)

I was active in the parents' association at the beginning. I needed the help more than. . . . Some had much more severe children than I did. I felt lucky to have Elizabeth. . . . Now I don't feel so sorry for myself. (M)

I belong to a parents' group. Sometimes it makes me feel good to see that Kathy's not as bad off as other children. (M)

Other parents, especially those whose children have the worst problems, remain active in associations, generally because full integration in normal society remains elusive to them:

I was in a mothers' group, but most of their children were Downs'. Compared to what Billy could do, they seemed like geniuses. . . . All of those kids have now "graduated" from (the program). I'm the oldest in the group now and the only one with teenage children. They're acquaintances more than friends. I have to bite my tongue there. I hear girls complaining who don't have a lot of problems. There is one little girl there with a lot of problems, and I do talk to her mother. (M)

The (Association) is our kids' only social life. . . . I'm on the board and I'm referee of the soccer team. This is the only way that we found that you could find out what's going on. . . . Most parents just pay dues in (the Association) but they don't come down. (F)

I'm friendly with other parents of the handicapped, but they don't have the same problems we do. . . . They complain to me about the problems they have with one child. They forget who they're talking to. (Laughs). (Respondent has four handicapped children.) (M)

I met other parents of the retarded after we moved here. I felt that made the biggest difference in my life. . . . Down there (where we lived before) with my husband working so much and no other families with retarded children I felt that I was just singled out for something, that I was weird. I felt a lot of isolation and bitterness. ...Meeting other parents you get practical hints — like how someone got their child to chew — that normal parents take for granted. (M)

For such parents, the seekership phase is a continuing status, because all of their needs are rarely ever met.

Another segment of the own consists of the other members of the nuclear family — the spouse and other children. In general, most parents felt that their child's handicap had made their family more cohesive. Almost all reported that other family members had been very supportive. The major complaint, where one existed, was that husbands sometimes left all of the seekership chores to their wives while they were involved in activities outside the home. (Such a complaint is, of course, typical of families without handicapped children as well.):

(My wife) is involved in quite a bit. I got to (an Association) meeting twice a year. I'm not involved socially with any of the people.

(My husband) buried himself in his work, and I had nothing. ...I wanted to run away. I was with Debbie all the time. I was isolated and lonely. I felt smothered.

I was not close with either of my children when they were young. I was in a big career buildup. ...(My wife) became involved in (the Association). I only went to meetings to support her.

A few mothers reported experiencing some kind of breakdown during their children's infancy, largely as a result of the pressure of having to care for and find help for their defective child entirely on their own. All reported an improvement in their mental state once they became part of parents' groups or other supportive networks.

The handicapped child's siblings are also part of the own, and most parents felt that the siblings were not adversely affected by the presence of the defective child. In some cases, the siblings were cast in the role of "protectors" of their brothers or sisters when other children taunted them, and a few reported incidents in which the siblings themselves were taunted:

> (My son) came home one day all upset because the kid down the street called Karen a "retard." He's very protective of her. (M)
>
> (My son's) friends ask, "What's wrong with your brother? How come he's so small?" He just says, "He's small because he didn't grow." (M)
>
> (Our older daughter) said once or twice that kids made fun of her because she had a retarded brother, but it isn't a problem now. Most people she knows are very accepting of him. (M)
>
> In school, occasionally a child will say, "I'm not going to sit next to you. Your brother's retarded," but it doesn't happen enough to discourage her from participating in school. (F)

Most of the parents felt that their other children had a good relationship with their handicapped siblings, even though they had been inconvenienced by them and had been left with babysitters frequently while their parents were at the hospital or were involved in various forms of seekership. Most parents begin socializing their other children early to understand and accept the problem. The following situation was reported by the mother of a Down's Syndrome infant:

> We recently met a family with a 12-year-old Down's, and our 9 year old asked, "Will Jeff look like that when he grows up?" I said, "He might," and she said, "Then don't tell anyone he's my brother." I tried to explain to her that that wasn't the right attitude.

In one case, older siblings were passed into service as part-time caretakers for their severely disabled brother. Their mother said that they rarely complained about their babysitting duties, and that she and her husband had made efforts to spend extra time with their normal children through scouting and special trips. She felt their added responsibilities were beneficial to them:

> I think my children will be better human beings. . . . They will be more understanding. . . more prepared for difficulties in life. . . more loving. (M)

This theme was echoed by several parents, who felt that their normal children would be more aware or more compassionate as a result of having a handicapped sibling.

In addition to intense interaction with spouse and other children, parents are also immersed in day-to-day interaction with handicapped children themselves. Such interaction is clearly important in shaping parents' definitions of the situation.

Many parents reported difficulties in simply providing physical care for their child in the early postpartum period. The most common problems involved feeding, and quite a few parents were frustrated by babies who would not eat. In some cases, feeding difficulties were complicated by various medical problems, so that the infant had seizures or vomited and cried constantly. The father of one such child said, "Susan seemed like a burden that was never going to end."

In a few cases, the child was hospitalized for long periods of time during infancy, delaying the possibility of a close parent-child relationship:

> She was never ours. At 3 weeks, we took her from _____ Hospital to _____ Children's Hospital. . . . We were commuting to the hospital three times a week from (a neighboring state), where my husband was stationed. . . . At 8 months

they handed her to me in a. . .cast. I was petrified. "How do I take care of this child?" (M)

The child's rate of development can also encourage or inhibit the relationship with parents. In general, a nonresponsive child is not as rewarding to parents as one who seems to thrive on or acknowledge parental efforts. Parents reported being discouraged, for example, by a baby who did not respond at all for the first 4 months and by one who still could not hold up her head at 3 years. Such feelings may be prolonged when a child has a very severe handicap: "Sometimes it smothers me. . . . It gets to be wearing when nothing ever changes in a child." (M)

The speed of development, however, is *not* necessarily a predictor of parental attitude. Some parents of very severely retarded youngsters still felt rewarded by the small accomplishments that their children *had* achieved, such as sitting up or grasping a toy. Typically, parents were relatively satisfied if their children seemed *happy*, regardless of their developmental level.

In some cases, parents reported being pleasantly surprised by their children:

They told me it would be a long hard road with nothing but heartaches. . . . It hasn't been that way at all. (M)

After what they told me, I expected just a little blob. I was surprised he was so normal. (M)

I'm surprised that she's developing like a normal baby. (M)

They told us he wouldn't walk, and I worried about it a lot because I have back problems and I couldn't carry him. Then, he started walking. (M)

We couldn't believe that she was so happy and healthy. . . . We were told very pessimistic things, like, "She'll never walk," "She might be retarded," "Death could come at any time." . . . She's not retarded, she can walk, she goes to regular school. . . . She started talking early. . . . By the time she was a year old, we were sure that she wasn't retarded, even though the doctors wouldn't say for sure. . . . We knew she would walk. . . . She had a table. . . that she pushed around the floor. The doctors didn't believe us. (M)

Other parents, whose children were still young, expressed fears that their youngsters might be retarded, or might not learn to walk or talk. Some mentioned that other children they knew had performed these skills at late ages and that they were hopeful that their children might do the same.

Comparisons, both favorable and unfavorable, with other children were commonly made by parents, although perhaps not to the extent that such comparing is done by parents of normal children. The unfavorable comparisons usually involved other children who were normal:

I see other 3 year olds, and they talk a mile a minute. (M)

I get very disappointed in (our 6 year old) when I see a little 3 year old come into the house. (F)

I had a friend who had a daughter who was born a week after Karen. We were pregnant together, we were in clubs together at that time, in church together. . . . This year. . . I kind of compared. I said, "Oh look at Jackie. You know, so much different. She's going to be a young lady, and Karen, you know, she's still really a baby compared to that." And I probably felt bad for a couple of weeks and then I forgot about it. . . . All of a sudden I noticed that Jackie had grown up and Karen hadn't. (M)

We have a 14-month-old nephew, and he's doing much more than Peter. (M)

I guess when he was a year old was when I started to get upset about it. That's when kids start walking, and he was still sitting in an infant seat. That's when people started justifiably avoiding me. . . because I was in such an emotional state they couldn't handle it. (M)

In other cases, parents compared their children favorably with others, either normal or handicapped:

He's just like any other kid. (F)

I would want another Down's child. I wouldn't have said that a year ago. ...So many (normal) kids turn out rotten. ...She'll never turn on us. (M)

I have a girlfriend with a baby born a month later than Peter, and Peter is on a higher level. (M)

You see kids a lot worse off. My kids could be sitting down and talking to you, and you'd never know there was anything wrong with them. (F)

Billy and (his brother) were easy to live with. They're not hyperactive or noisy like some children. (F)

Unlike a lot of retarded children, he's cute. And he's no trouble. (M)

She's small but she's attractive. Have you seen _____ (another family's severely retarded child)? He really looks repulsive. Susan's looks have helped her socially. (F)

I thought she was beautiful. ...She didn't have that "retarded look." (M)

Although my kids are — you know — handicapped, if you saw them sitting down, you probably wouldn't realize that they couldn't get up to walk. They don't have any — you know — what's the word — uh — it's not that obvious, you know. And — did you see the children? (Interviewer: "I met the boys.") They're nice looking kids. I mean they don't have any disfigurement, you know, so I think when you see my kids compared to some cerebral palsies. (M)

These favorable comparisons might be regarded by some as rationalizations. However, parents of normal children (including those in the check sample in this study) commonly engage in similar comparison between their children and those of other parents.

When parents were asked directly about the development of their relationship with their handicapped children, many noted a change over time. While quite a few parents wished their children would die during early infancy, all felt that the frequency and intensity of parent-child interaction had favored the growth of love, especially as the child began to respond socially in any manner at all:

She's my baby, and I love her and I wouldn't trade her for another child. (M)

I love him. I don't know what I'd do without him. (M)

We have a good relationship. Jimmy can be fun. (M)

They're very happy kids. . . . This family is closer together than anything. (F)

I can't imagine life without her. . . . The thing I dread most is her death. We know we will lose her someday, and that is the worst thing. (F)

It's hard to imagine life without Julie. She's part of the family. . . . She's as much one of our family as any of them. (M)

She's my whole world. (M)

Liz and I are very close. She knows that I'll always be there when she's sick or needs me. . . . This kid is my life. (M)

It's taken me two years to adjust to her. I've come a long way emotionally. . . . Now I wouldn't trade her for any child in the world. (M)

Most parents felt that their children fit in well with the normal routine of family life. As one father said, "Retardation is not number one around this house. It's just something that Karen has." Some, whose children were retarded, simply continued to define their offspring as "babies" and treat them accordingly well into childhood. The difficulties in these cases were those common to families with normal babies: sleep and feeding problems, relatively large amounts of time devoted to child care, and especially, limitations on parents' freedom of movement:

> If there's ever a tag-along, she's the one....She's fast. The grandmothers can't really keep up with her. ...We don't let her out alone. She can't join in the older children's games. They realize she can't keep up. (F)

> We can't just pick up and do something. A lot of times we say, "What will we do with Michelle?" (M)

> I won't leave her with a sitter because she won't eat. (M)

> Normally, if I go away for a weekend, say a very economical weekend, $150 let's say, for both of us. ...I would have to, on top of that, pay somebody $45 to stay with my kids, and when you come home, the house is total disaster. It's that kind of a battle. (F)

> If you can even *find* somebody to stay with the kids. ...I don't care what we do — we always have to sit down and think about it: "How are we going to get there on time?" (M)

> We don't get out much. This year is the first time we got away for vacation. (F)

> We always have to plan around Billy. We have to think, "Now we're taking Billy with us, what kinds of problems are we going to get into? What do we have to prepare for?" We can't just pick up and go someplace. (F)

> I always have to be home when his school bus arrives. (M)

> When Susan was 7 months old, I had to go away, so I called Mrs. _____ (another mother with an extremely handicapped child, whom this respondent had never met), and she recommended a sitter. I said, "She cries and she vomits. Just do the best you can." ...When I got there I called home, and the sitter said that Susan was crying and vomiting. ...She finally fell asleep. That first time was the hardest. After that, I wasn't as afraid to leave her. (M)

> It's hard to get babysitters. ...One woman I use is 76 years old, but I can only use her after he's asleep, because she can't lift him. (M)

He's hard to take with us. I always have to get a babysitter or I'll stay home. ...It's really like having a little baby, only he doesn't outgrow it. ...And we don't as a rule have people over — because he doesn't go to sleep. (M)

He requires so much of our time, which limits our social life considerably. And it's a permanent thing. Anything we might do is limited by Brian's need for our physical presence. (F)

One thing that does bother me about going out — she's not toilet-trained. ...I can't go in the Ladies' room and I can't bring her in the Men's room. ...You should be able to take a 7 year old and say, "Go to the bathroom; we're going to be in the car for awhile." (F)

Prolonged "infancy" can thus be quite frustrating to parents. A normal infant is *expected* to be a burden; a normal older child is not. Parents must therefore redefine their expectations in the case of a retarded child.

Another factor in parents' definitions of their children, when the children are sufficiently old or intelligent to have a self-concept, is the children's definitions of themselves. The following are the experiences/self-definitions, as perceived by parents, of some of the school-age children of normal or near-normal intelligence in the sample:

In the beginning, he was very bitter that he had to be taken out of contact sports. ...He was being regularly beat up because he wouldn't tell the kids why he couldn't be in gym. He tried to share it with a close friend of his, and this friend has since made fun of him. So I think that hurt Jimmy a lot. I asked him if kids make fun of him in the showers at school. He said, "They hadn't better." ...He can handle it....He has said he would like his brain in a different body. (M)

Jean would like a boyfriend. ...She will sometimes say, "Oh, somebody stopped to talk to me today (in school)," and that makes her very happy. There isn't much mingling with the normal kids. ...She gets upset if someone says, "Have you always been in a wheelchair?'' or ''How long do you have to stay in a wheelchair?'' (M)

> She's asked questions pretty steadily. She thinks she will throw away her braces when she grows up. . . . She asks, ''Why do I have to wear diapers like babies? Why can't I go to the beach?'' I tell her, ''If you didn't wear diapers, I wouldn't have you. I'm very glad you wear diapers.'' . . . Her biggest problem with other kids is the diapers. They call her ''baby.'' . . . She has a group of close friends who stay around her, and they stick up for her. . . . (The mother is pregnant.) I asked her how she would feel if the baby were normal, and she said, ''I can do anything the baby can do, only slower.'' So I think it's going to be all right. (M)

All of the parents felt that, although their school-age children had concerns related to their handicaps, they were basically happy and reasonably well adjusted to their situation.

Within the nuclear family, then, members seem to be able to adapt, sometimes with difficulty, to the problems created by a handicapped child. If anything, the presence of such a child seems to draw family members closer together as an in-group facing the hostilities of the outside world. Several parents cited this cohesion as a positive effect of the child's presence at home. As one mother said,

> All of us have gained a certain awareness and a certain compassion. I can see it in (my normal daughter). . . . It's deepened the relationship between (my husband) and myself. Coming across a problem that can't be solved is a maturing thing.

The literature of course cites families torn apart by the presence of a handicapped child. (Such families are often weak *prior* to the birth of such a child.) The data of this study suggest that such an effect is by no means a necessary consequences of this situation and that, in fact, an opposite effect may be just as likely.

While acceptance may occur fairly smoothly in the nuclear family, acceptance by the extended family is quite variable. Some parents reported relatives who were very loving, sympathetic, and helpful, while others noted that their families were distant and stigmatizing, to varying degrees. In the sample as a whole, helpful relatives generally prevailed, especially in the role of babysitters for the handicapped child. Grandparents also provided financial aid to help cover the expenses of medical care. In one case, relatives said that they would take their retarded niece into their home if anything ever happened to her parents. In another case, a grandmother sewed all the special-size diapers needed by her granddaughter.

In some cases, reactions from relatives were mixed:

My mother has always been very loving towards him. She holds him the whole time. (My husband's) mother has never held him. . . . (Other relatives) don't want to get involved at all. (M)

Lack of involvement was a fairly common complaint about various extended family members (although such complaints existed in the normal sample as well):

I care very much about the way may parents feel about Susan. They don't get as involved as I would like. (F)

One of the things I resented about my mother was that she would treat Julie differently from (our normal son). . . overly affectionate but not genuine. (M)

I wish my sister would get more involved with her. (M)

In the case of the family with four handicapped children, relatives were relatively supportive at first, but by the time the fourth child was diagnosed, the parents were blamed rather than supported:

I didn't get much support from anyone (in my husband's family). All I got was criticism. It was as though I was a lady of the street and went out and became pregnant.

We've been pretty much on our own. . . . Our family thought we were crazy. (F)

When relatives react negatively, they are generally dropped from the parents' reference set rather than influencing parental attitudes unfavorably. In these cases, supportive friends and neighbors are occasionally substituted as significant others. More commonly, the nuclear family simply falls back on its own resources, and its members support one another.

Another major area of seekership outside the family is the quest for appropriate educational or training programs. In a few cases of recently born children, parents were directed to "infant stimulation" programs early by a knowledgeable pediatrician. In the large majority of cases, however, parents reported lengthy and difficult searches or crusades before they obtained satisfactory schooling for their children. In some cases, satisfactory schooling is never obtained.

The following is an example of a successful quest in this area:

We were in the _____ Regional Center area. They said when he was 3 years old, they would take him in a program. . . . Then I found out they would take him just fine but there was no way of getting there, and it was a 45 minute drive for me each way, and I had a kindergartener who was only gone two hours. . . . So I would have had to stay there or spend my whole life in the car. There was a bus that would have taken him but it would have been two hours one way and three hours the other, because we were at the very end of the line. . . . That's when I decided, "If he's going to have school, we're going to have to move." . . .

It was very difficult to get information. I called the state agencies, but they didn't give me anything. I finally had to go to every single town, every director of special ed., in the (city)

area, and I visited just about every pre-school that they had.
. . . Just about every one I went to, there were some little kids
sitting nicely, learning about their colors and shapes and
everything. . . and there was this one little kid crawling around
in the corner playing with the wastebasket. That was very
typical, and I knew that that was Brian. Until I went to see
these schools, I didn't know where Brian ranked in the hierar-
chy of the retarded. . . .

If you live in _____ and have a handicapped child, you
move, because they don't have any programs. . . . I wasn't going to be the one that fought the system. . . .

At _____ Program, the profoundly retarded were being
shown books. . . . They weren't just left in a corner. . . . We
could have afforded to live elsewhere more easily, but we
moved to _____, because that's where the _____ Program
was. (M)

In other cases, parents *did* fight the system:

In her old school, Karen had been in the same (trainable) class
for three or four years. There were toys in the room. . . . The
trainable teacher had been trying to teach Karen and a few
others to read, but the special education director they had at
the time said, "No, these children can't read." . . . A
psychologist had once told us that Karen would be able to
read some day, and she wanted to learn.

(After awhile) we didn't think that Karen would get any
more out of the trainable class. We begged them to test her.
. . . We petitioned the Board. . . . A psychologist from the
state said, "She's not ready." I felt like crying. Karen was a
lot dumber than I thought she was. . . .

(A year later) we had her tested by a private psychologist.
. . . He said that her speech needed improvement but that her
vocabulary was almost normal rather than retarded. . . . He
thought she should be in the educable class. . . . They finally
moved her. . . . She's been in the educable class for a year now
and she's (doing the work). She may always be in that class,
but at least she's learning something again. (M)

The most remarkable story was told by the parents of four handicapped teenagers, whose combination of problems was so unique that they did not fit into *any* established educational program:

At _____ Children's Hospital, Tony was in a class with active, bright kids. ...He just sat in the corner and played in the sandbox. ...Then, he went to _____ School for the Blind, which is geared for the totally blind child (Tony had some vision). They mostly concentrated on teaching Braille. Finally, Tony and Jean had to leave the school. They said they were retarded. ...The teachers there were not trained in learning disabilities. With each of our children, we were told, "Tony couldn't do it, so you can't expect Jean to do it," or "Jean couldn't do it, so you can't expect Richie to do it." (M)

They weren't really blind. They were multiply handicapped. (F)

The teachers are better trained now. Our children are learning something for the first time. Years ago we were told our children couldn't learn. ...It's been a constant fight just getting the appropriate education for these kids....

After Tony and Jean were labeled retarded by the _____ School for the Blind, they started in the (city) Public School System, but they had no appropriate program either. ...After three years, we started fighting. ...The Board of Education said, "We've got all kinds of retarded programs. We'll just put them in one of those." ...I visited the programs, and there wasn't one child in a wheelchair. ...I said, "How are my children going to get around? How are they going to go on these stairs?..." They kept saying "No" to us....

We were lucky at this time, because (my husband) was in the school system and he knew a lot of people. And they were guiding us and telling us where to write, each step of the way. We went right to the top. ...A program was established within two weeks....

They had told us we had the only multiply handicapped teenagers in the city of _____. I said, "We have the only *siblings*, but you've got a lot of *misplaced* multiply handicapped children." I knew them all....

Now the program is getting bigger, and we're still fighting. We need more class space. (M)

They've got two places for the handicapped, no matter what school you go to. They're either in the cellar or in the attic. They're never in with the other kids. ...Our kids are kept downstairs because the fire regulations state that they need a monitor to carry them downstairs in case of fire. ...Everyone's afraid to stick their neck out. The teachers just do their job. (F)

I really feel our kids would be much further ahead if they had the right training from the beginning. (M)

A lot more could be done. Our 15 year old is in an industrial arts workshop now. He's good at carpentry. ...We tried to get them to do that with Tony 10 years ago. ...Tony is 19, and we don't know what he can do. (F)

In other cases, parental crusades were not nearly as long-lasting, because solutions were generally found relatively early — parents called the Association for the Retarded and were immediately told of a good local program or they were referred to such a program by a social worker or other professional. In one case, a child was not enrolled in a program, because her mother had no car and could not get her there. In another case, a child of normal intelligence with impaired vision was placed in a class with severely retarded children. Her problems were solved, however, when she was moved to a normal nursery school.

In several cases, parents noted that their place of residence, and consequently, their job, was dictated to some extent by the availability of good special education facilities. Two fathers in the sample had in fact changed jobs as a direct result of their children's problems. In one case, the father left a job that involved frequent transfers, and in the other, the father went to work for the school system in an attempt to be in a better position to demand the facilities and programs his children needed.

In general, most parents had high praise for special education teachers. Of all the professionals with whom these parents must interact, teachers receive the most credit and respect for having helped these children and their parents by teaching important skills. Another positive feature of special education programs, *for parents*, is that they allow overburdened parents some free time. As one mother said, "When Billy started at _____, it was the first time I had two hours to go grocery shopping during the day."

Although reactions to teachers were generally favorable, reactions to other helping professionals and societal agencies were not. As one mother said, "Our society is not geared for the retarded. We used to send them all away and now we don't know what to do with them." A common experience reported by parents was one of being blamed rather than helped by societal agents, of being made to feel that because *they* had given birth to a defective child, *they* should somehow provide for their children's unusual educational, physical, or other needs. When parents have difficulty providing these things that parents of normal children take for granted, they are sometimes accused of being neurotic or are defined as bad parents.

Sometimes, professionals do not take into account conditions in a child's home because they are far removed from the context of the day-to-day family situation. The parents of four handicapped teenagers mentioned earlier, for example, noted that they are constantly being chided for not helping their children dress themselves for school. With just one handicapped child in a family, such reproach might be reasonable. However, trying to help four children with poor motor coordination all at the same time might be an impossible task.

Instead, these parents have established a division of labor in which each parent dresses two children each morning.

The same family also has difficulty doing anything as a family because of the impossibility of manipulating four wheelchairs at once. The mother reported that as a special treat, the family had recently gone together to a friend's restaurant for dinner. The next day, the mother was criticized for allowing her overweight daughter to "indulge" in a full-course Italian meal. The mother complained to the interviewer, "You can't even lead your own life." The family has managed to maintain a sense of humor, however, and the parents are able to joke about their situation. They laugh about strangers who assume, on the rare occasions that they are able to go out as a family, that they are paid or volunteer aides on an institutional outing rather than the parents of their own children.

This mother (and several others in the samples) reported having seen various therapists to help adjust to the problems created by a handicapped child. This mother said that she had a "nervous breakdown" after her fourth handicapped child was born. She also had a "weight problem" and went to a psychologist for help:

> I told my doctor I was always tired, and he said, "It's your nerves." ...It got to the point where I thought, "Nobody wants to help me." ...I saw a psychologist on TV. ...and I called him...He said, "Don't you think someone else could take care of your children as well as you can?" I said, "It's not a matter of someone else. It's a matter of being able to pay somebody." ...He said, "Go to work." ...I'm not qualified. I've been home for 20 years. ...I'm seeing someone else now. He's kind of giving me the blame for the way I am: "It's your fault you feel the way you do about things." I don't want to feel this way. ...He says, "You create your own problems." My problem is that I have four handicapped

children, and that has nothing to do with the fact that I had an unhappy childhood. . . . I'm nervous because I have reason to be nervous. . . . That night we were supposed to go someplace, and the van at the CP Center broke down, so suddenly we had four kids to worry about. . . . We had to change our plans. . . . That's the problem with these professionals. . . . They have a job. . . . They don't live with the parents 24 hours a day. What sounds nice at the office just doesn't work in real life.[5]

In order to deal with their problems, when help from society is not forthcoming, many of these families become child-centered, in an attempt to meet their children's needs on their own. An extreme example of such an adaptation is presented, once again, by the family with four handicapped children. The father explained,

State aid is based on one handicap per family. I wrote to the governor and said, "I have four handicapped kids," but I didn't get any help. . . . Our kids have a phone. It's essential. Other kids go out and play. We can't afford it but we have it. . . . We also can't afford the swimming pool, but water's the best therapy. . . . Where else can they go and swim almost every day in the summer? The city don't have it, so I have it. . . . The pool is heated and it's only three and a half to four and a half feet deep (chuckles)—my wife's a nonswimmer. It's the best thing in the world for them. If you dress them before they go in and you dress them after, you can see how much good it's done. . . .

If they want to go someplace, you've got to take them. I've got a van out there that cost me over $8000. Normally, you could buy that van for $5500. It cost me $1300 for a lift. I had to get the seats cut and reupholstered. . . . It's for the kids. Everything we do is for the kids.

This family had thus created, at great expense, and individualistic solution to some of their problems. On a more altruistic level, these parents were active in the local cerebral palsy association, so that other children as well as their own, could have a social life outside the home.

Altruistic solutions were also employed by other parents in the sample, particularly in cases of children with the most severe handicaps. These parents were the most acutely aware of the lack of societal resources for the handicapped. Thus, one mother was involved in compiling a directory of available training programs and other resources for new parents of handicapped children. Other parents were involved in setting up a peer counseling service, in which experienced parents of handicapped children were being trained to visit other parents who had recently given birth to a defective child.

Beginning in their child's infancy, then, parents of defective children must search and fight for the services that parents of normal children take for granted: medical care, education, social acceptance, freedom of movement. Some writers attribute such searching and fighting to guilt. However, such parental behavior is as easily understandable within the context of parents' trying to "do their job" as parents in an inhospitable society.

PROBLEMS WITHOUT SOLUTIONS: WHEN SEEKERSHIP ENDS

Parents generally leave the active seekership role when they have obtained satisfactory medical, educational, social, and other needed services for their children. For parents whose children's handicaps are fairly common or not severe, the quest is usually a short one. Such families generally establish a normalized routine fairly early, and their lifestyle probably does not differ significantly from that of a family with only normal children. Some of their friends may have handicapped children, but most of their friends do not. Even families with severely handicapped children can maintain a normalized lifestyle if they receive enough social support. A good example of such a family is the one with a spina bifida daughter discussed in previous sections. This family had very supportive relatives, who babysat, sewed diapers. and provided help in other ways. The school system was also supportive, and the child, although severely handicapped and incontinent, went to a normal nursery school and then a regular public school. Limitations on the family's lifestyle were thus relatively minor, such as having to avoid tourist attractions with stairs.

Other families were not so fortunate. Some had children whose medical condition, mobility, or behavior problems forced them to limit family activities, especially when competent babysitters were not available:

> Nobody's (relatives) ever said, "We'll take the kids for a week so you can get away." Some friends have offered but their house won't accommodate a wheelchair. (M)

> We often have not done something because of the inconvenience Billy would make to other people. (F)

> There are things we'd like to do with (our two normal children). We'd like to take some trips before (our daughter) goes to college. In another year she'll be in college. . . . But we can't do that now. . . . It's hard to travel with Billy now. . . . Because of his medical problems, I'm fearful to leave. I don't want to end up in a strange hospital somewhere. Everyone knows Billy at University Hospital now, and that's very relieving. (M)

In a few cases, parents felt that their family size had been limited by the presence of the handicapped child. As one mother explained, "I was going to have another baby, but then Allison kept getting sick. . . . If I had another child, one would be neglected."

Another burden noted by a number of parents was the continuing financial problem created by a handicapped child:

> We're always in debt. . . . We just keep paying _____ Children's Hospital a little bit every month. (F)

My biggest worry is that if anything should happen to me, I want her to be treated right, so money is very important. (F)

When you have a handicapped child, everything is so expensive. Wheelchairs, crutches...it's such a rip-off. ...Richie wears out a pair of shoes a month. (M)

We spend so much on babysitters. ...There should be some type of supplemental income for people who keep children like this at home. (M)

For a few families, continuing medical problems prolonged the seekership phase in this area. In two cases, parents had recently learned that their chldren required further surgery. Other parents feared that surgery might be required in the future, and in a small number of cases, where a child's condition had been diagnosed as ultimately fatal, parents were concerned about, although not generally obsessed with, their child's death. In one case, where the child's death was imminent, the parents had resigned themselves to their fate and, while they would continue medical treatment to the end, they had abandoned any new attempts at seekership.

All of the parents, whether they had established a normalized routine or were still in the process of adjusting to an abnormal one, had one insoluble problem in common: What would happen to their child in the future? These parents had, for the most part, neutralized their concern by adopting a philosophy of living one day at a time. However, most admitted worrying about who would care for their child if something happened to them. Most admitted the possibility of institutionalization, although they were not in favor of it. As one mother said, "I know what those institutions are like. If you're low-functioning, you don't do anything." Several parents hoped that their children would be able to avoid institutionalization by entering a community-based facility such as a group home or sheltered workshop. Most parents feared, however, that the number of such facilities would be insufficient to meet future needs. In all cases, however, parents intended to keep their handicapped children at home for as long as possible.

Most parents emphatically stated that they would not want their normal children to be burdened with their handicapped siblings, and that other family members would not want the burden. In one case, however, relatives had assured the parents that they would care for their retarded daughter, and in a few other cases, siblings had insisted, despite their parents' protests, that they would take care of their handicapped brothers and/or sisters.

Although most parents were hesitant to discuss the future, when prodded, the majority revealed realistic hopes and fears and modest expectations:

I hope to see him take care of himself someday. (M)

There was a Down's woman who was a dishwasher at work. My first rection was, "My daughter will not wash dishes for somebody else." Later, I thought, "Well, maybe she'd like washing dishes." I just want her to do whatever she wants to do. (M)

I'm grateful he's bright. Even though he won't be able to do manual labor, he'll always be able to do some type of work. (M)

I don't care if my children are not "smart." I just want them to be able to carry on a conversation so they won't be shut off in a corner somewhere. (M)

She likes to mimic so she may be able to pick up some kind of trade. (M)

I would like her to learn to read. (M)

We know that, medically, Billy is not in the future. (M)

I just want her to live and be happy. (M)

We'll never reach the stage that other people reach when their children leave home, and that's depressing. . . . I also wonder what will happen to Brian when he no longer looks like a child. (F)

I don't want to think about her adolescence, when the other girls will be dating. . . . It will be hard for her. (M)

I'm afraid that children will tease her. (F)

All of the parents were asked a hypothetical question at the end of the interview: If you had some way of knowing, *before* you (your wife) became pregnant with (child's name) that he/she would have this problem, knowing what you do now, do you think you would have wanted him/her to be born?[6] (The question was phrased in this way to avoid the issue of abortion.) The majority of answers were negative, for a number of reasons:

No, I wouldn't have wanted her. She has limited our lifestyle. . . . She is a burden and a heartbreak. (F) (Child has Down's Syndrome)

No. Why bring a child into this world who's going to be handicapped? He's going to be ridiculed. There'll be pain. . . . I don't think it's fair to bring any child into this world who's going to suffer. (F) (Down's Syndrome)

I'm not sorry. I think it's opened a whole new world for me —you don't get involved until it strikes home. . . . I think, once I conceived a Down's child, I would have it. But I probably wouldn't intentionally conceive one. (M)

I'm closer to him than to any of my children and I love him desperately. But I wouldn't have had him. I wouldn't condemn a child to that. It's not for us; it's for him. (M) (rare genetic syndrome)

I wouldn't have another like Nicole. I love her, but it's not fair for her to go through all that. I would rather have her than no child at all. But I would rather have a normal child. (M) (rare genetic syndrome)

I wouldn't have conceived her. I love her but I would have preferred a normal child. (M) (Down's Syndrome)

I wouldn't want her to be taken away, even if we could be given a new baby but I'm in favor of abortion. I don't think a child should be born with a strike against them. (F) (Down's Syndrome)

Yes, I would want her. But I wouldn't want another. (Our daughter) is so good, so healthy. It would be easy to have her over again. But another one might not be like that. (M) (Down's Syndrome)

I would not have wanted him to be born I would not have wanted to be committed to this. (F) (multiple severe handicaps)

Just because he's not complete doesn't mean he doesn't have rights as a person. He's definitely a person. I would not have had an abortion. I guess the only reason I wouldn't have had him is that he's had a lot of pain. ...I don't think any child should have to go through that. ...It's made us better people. (M) (multiple severe handicaps)

The benefits have outweighed the drawbacks. There have been a lot of positive factors. I would probably have had an abortion if I had known. ...His handicap is too severe. If he died now, I would grieve. (M) (cerebral palsy)

I would not have wanted him to be born. It would have improved the quality of the rest of our lives. I don't think that _____ gets that much out of life. (F) (cerebral palsy)

I probably wouldn't have wanted her to be born. I wouldn't want anything to happen to her now. (M) (retarded)

At first, I couldn't see any good at all out of (his birth). ...It has made us better people. We've learned a lot from the experience but we wouldn't have knowingly gone through it. (M) (Down's Syndrome)

I would not have another child with this problem. I wouldn't go through it again—and for her sake. ...I wouldn't want to bring any deformed child into the world. (M) (eye problem)

I wouldn't have another CP child. I've had enough trouble with _____. ...If I had to have no children at all or have _____ the way she is, I would rather have _____, but I would rather have a normal child. (M)

Most parental responses to the question were mixed. Although the majority would not have burdened their children with their problems, they felt that *they* would have missed a positive experience if their children had not been born. *All* of the parents said that they would have preferred a normal child but that they had grown to love the defective child they had.

Approximately one-fifth of the parents in the sample answered the question affirmatively, without qualification. Some of their answers follow:

> She's my baby and I love her and I wouldn't trade her for another child. . . . They told me it would be a long hard road with nothing but heartaches. . . . It hasn't been that way at all. (M) (Down's Syndrome)

> I wouldn't have amniocentesis. That would be like admitting you didn't want a Down's child. I don't think they're that bad off. (F)

> I would want another Down's child. I wouldn't have said that a year ago. So many kids turn out rotten. . . . She'll never turn on us. (M)

> If I had a choice I would still want her—but I would rather have a normal child. (M) (multiple severe handicaps)

> I don't regret having _____. I can't imagine life without her. (F) (eye problem)

> If I knew it would turn out the way it did, I would have had her. But if her problem would have been worse, . . . probably not. (F) (eye problem)

> I don't see how *anyone* can say in the first two hours after birth what the quality of your life is going to be. Elizabeth has enriched our life. I wouldn't change it for the world. . . . Elizabeth has taught me love and patience and how to give of myself. (This mother is pregnant and has not had amniocentesis. She would rather have another spina bifida child than no other child. She is also opposed to intentionally allowing a spina bifida baby to die after birth.) It's my baby and I don't want any doctors deciding what will happen to it.

Positive responses tended to be very slightly more common among mothers than fathers.

Thus, parental careers show many similarities as well as marked differences. In general, response to an unfavorable social context in these cases involves a period of parental activism, which declines as solutions are discovered or created. Several career types emerge with some clarity from the data. The two that are the clearest and most typical of the sample are the "personal seekers" and the "crusaders." These are presented below.

Ideal Types and Representative Cases

PERSONAL SEEKERS

The majority of parents in the sample more or less approximate a type characterized by the following process:

(1) Postpartum amonie, marked by a strong need for information (meaning) and direction (power or control over one's own situation), followed by:

(2) Satisfaction of the need for meaning but continuation of the need for direction (the "plateau phase"), followed fairly soon by:

(3) A seekership phase, in which direction is actively sought, followed by:

(4) The discovery of solutions (the "revelation phase"), followed by:

(5) The establishment of a normalized routine (the "normalization phase").

The process of movement from one phase to another is best illustrated by the presentation of cases in their entirety. Two cases that closely represent the personal seeker type follow:

CASE   20

Background. The father is a 35-year-old electrical contractor, high school graduate, from a medium-sized northeastern city, has one sibling. The mother is a 33-year-old part-time X-ray technician from a small town near a large Eastern metropolis, has two siblings. The family is Protestant. The parents have been married for 13 years and have an 11-year-old son and a 7-year-old son in addition to a daughter, 10-year-old Karen, an attractive and personable child with Down's Syndrome. The family owns a home in a small town that is part of a medium-sized metropolitan area.

The Prenatal Period. These parents were eager to have children, and Karen was born just 17 months after her brother. They anticipated the birth of a normal child. The father had never heard of Down's Syndrome, and the mother, who had seen institutionalized adults, had a very negative view of the condition. The couple was close to their families, who were very supportive during the pregnancy.

Birth/Postpartum Anomie. The mother was first informed of her daughter's problem by a doctor who "hemmed and hawed" before he finally revealed what was wrong. The mother told her husband. Both were shocked and upset but decided not to tell family members because the wife's sister was expecting a baby. This secrecy increased their feelings of isolation.

The Plateau Phase. The father looked the condition up in the dictionary and then called the doctor, who told him to make an application for training school. The parents did not like the idea of institutionalization, however. The mother went to the library and did some research to satisfy her need for information.

The Seekership Phase. Relatives were finally told of the problem when the baby was 4 months old. The family was supportive, although the husband's mother kept saying "She'll get better."

The parents heard about the Association for the Retarded and became active members. They also became friendly with another family with a Down's child through the Association. Eventually, Karen went to the Association's nursery school and later to a special class in the public school.

The parents finally left their pediatrician, who kept insisting that they "leave it up to the doctor when it comes time to put her in an institution." They found a new doctor who "takes the time to talk to you" and like him much better.

After Karen had been in the trainable class at school for three or four years, her parents felt she was ready to be moved to the educable class. A battle with the school system ensued, until finally, the parents had Karen tested by a private psychologist. His findings were accepted, and Karen was moved to the educable class, where she was doing well at the time of the interview.

The Revelation Phase. The wife's mother moved in with the family, ending any babysitter problems that might have existed. Relatives said that if anything ever happened to Karen's parents, they would take care of her. The parents continued to be satisfied with Karen's medical care and school placement. Friends, neighbors, and strangers were found to be "so accepting." Karen remained healthy and continued to develop well in most areas.

The Normalization Phase. The parents are no longer active in the Association for the Retarded, nor do they see other families with retarded children socially. Karen gets along normally with her siblings and has friends in the neighborhood. Her friends are normal, although considerably younger than she is. The family camps and engages in other normal activities. As the father says, "Retardation is not number one around here. It's just something that Karen has."

CASE   15

Background. The father is a 28-year-old high school graduate from a small Eastern town, has one sibling. The mother is a 27-year-old high school graduate from an Eastern metropolitan area, has two siblings. The family is Protestant. They have a landscaping business and live above the husband's mother's general store in a small Eastern town near a large state university. The couple has been married eight years and has one living child, Elizabeth, age 6, who was born with myelomeningocele/hydrocephalus (spina bifida). Elizabeth is a friendly child who wears braces and walks with crutches. She is incontinent. The mother was pregnant at the time of the interview.

The Prenatal Period. The parents had always wanted children and were happy about the pregnancy. Both families were supportive. In the middle of the fourth month of pregnancy, the husband left for Viet Nam, and the wife went to live with her mother. The wife was worried that the baby might be deformed because she was not very active as a fetus.

Birth/Postpartum Anomie. The wife's mother was with her in the labor room. The baby was delivered by an emergency Caesarean Section after the mother started hemorrhaging. She had had only spinal anesthesia, but when the baby was born "they said, 'Oh my God, put her out'." When she awoke, a surgical consent was thrust at her, and she was told only that the baby had "something too much to talk about." No one would give her any information about the baby, who had been moved to another hospital, and she felt very depressed.

The husband was sent home from Viet Nam on emergency leave, because both his wife and child were in critical condition, and was very supportive once he arrived. When the wife was discharged from the hospital after 10 days, they went straight to the hospital where the baby was being kept. The wife was "petrified" at the thought of seeing her baby for the first time.

The Plateau Phase. Once they saw the baby, the couple finally received an explanation of her condition from the doctors. They held her and fed her and began getting attached to her. The "honeymoon" was shortlived, however. At three weeks, they took the baby from the hospital where she had had her first surgery to a children's hospital, where she would undergo a lengthy series of orthopedic, neurosurgical, and urological procedures. At the time, the parents were not completely aware of the nature of the procedures or of the various complications that might develop. They felt that, for the moment, their daughter's treatment was "out of their hands."

The Seekership Phase. The baby was in the hospital for eight months, and despite her numerous problems, she thrived. Relatives thought the baby was "fantastic" and were very supportive.

After the initial hospitalization, the family continued to take their daughter back and forth to the hospital for further surgery, cast fittings, and other procedures. The parents began to feel that doctors were running their life. At one point, a doctor had insisted that Elizabeth enter the hospital to lose weight. Although she had been placed on a strict diet, Elizabeth left the hospital two pounds heavier than when she entered—the nurses had felt sorry for her and fed her extra amounts. After this experience, the parents were particularly distrustful of doctors, and they began to take more and more of an initiative in directing their daughter's medical care. They also became active in the spina bifida parents' association at this time and became close to several individual parents in the group.

The Relevation Phase. Even though she had mobility problems and was incontinent, Elizabeth was accepted at a normal nursery school, and then in a regular class at public school. She is well accepted by the other children.

The family is highly supportive and will babysit so that the parents can take short vacations.

Elizabeth's medical condition has apparently stabilized, so that hospital visits, particularly inpatient stays, are much less frequent now. Some medical problems remain, but the parents feel that they are more in control now.

The Normalization Phase. The family maintains a relatively normal lifestyle, with minor modifications—Elizabeth has difficulty walking on certain surfaces and cannot climb stairs.

Although Elizabeth has some friends at "myelo" clinic, she does not see them outside. "They live too far away," and the mother will not "go out of her way" because she wants her daughter to be "as normal as possible." Thus, all of Elizabeth's friends are normal.

The parents are no longer active in the parents' association. Rather, they are preoccupied with the normal concerns of running a business, wanting to buy a house, and preparing for their new baby.

CRUSADERS

Most of the remaining parents in the sample approximated a type that resembles the personal seeker career in its first three phases: postpartum anomie, plateau, and seekership. However, revelation tends to be replaced by a permanent "crusade," because no solutions generally exist for the problems these families face. Personal seekership suggests that solutions are already available, even though parents may have to search and fight to obtain them. Parents embark on crusades when, after all avenues of seekership have been exhausted, they discover that no appropriate solutions exist. Crusades thus involve a quest for social change in an attempt to create solutions. Seekership, then, is a process of discovery, while crusadership is a process of invention. The latter process is also conducive to the formation of social movements, as private crusades join and become public. The following cases illustrate the crusadership career:

CASE 19

Background. The father is a 44-year-old engineering supervisor, a high school graduate, from an Eastern metropolitan area, has one sibling. The mother is a 38-year-old college graduate with a degree in nursing, from a small town in the East, with no siblings. The family is Protestant. The parents have been married for 17 years and have two living children, 16-year-old Mary and 13-year-old Bobby, in addition to 9-and-a-half-year-old Billy, who is severely brain damaged. Billy is extremely small for his age and quite deformed. He is able to sit with support and appears to have some awareness of his surroundings, although he is unable to communicate. The parents also had two other defective children, a daughter who died at 10 days and a son, two years younger than Billy, who died at 3 years. The family owns a home in a suburb of a large Eastern city.

The Prenatal Period. The parents had wanted a large family and were happy about the pregnancy. Both parents had some knowledge of handicaps since the husband's father was physically handicapped and the mother had worked as a nurse. However, they did not anticipate that their unborn child would have any problems.

Birth/Postpartum Anomie. The mother was aware, from the rections of the delivery room staff, that something was wrong with her baby. However, the problem was labeled only as "birth defects." The baby was kept in an isolette in the back of the nursery, and the mother felt that she was ignored by the hospital staff. She was disturbed that the pediatrician did not remember her or her daughter who had died. The baby was discharged without a diagnosis, and the parents were instructed to take him to a large hospital in another city. After two weeks, he was discharged, in worse medical condition than when he entered, with a diagnosis only of "congenital defects." The parents were told to put him in an institution and forget about him.

The Plateau Phase. The mother knew from her nursing experience that Billy would not survive in an institution, so the parents brought Billy home. The family's pediatrician continued to pressure the parents to put Billy in an institution. The mother became frustrated as she cared for the baby at home when he did not respond at all.

The Seekership Phase. The mother was aware of a Philadelphia-based program called patterning, in which a defective child is subjected to intensive stimulation in order to evoke response. She had been a volunteer, helping to pattern a child in another town prior to Billy's birth. Hence, she began to think of patterning when Billy did not develop at all. The parents undertook the rigorous patterning program against the advice of their pediatrician. They did not feel that patterning would provide a cure, but rather, felt the need to "*do* something" for Billy.

The wife's mother gave them the money, they left their older children with friends, and they made the trip to Philadelphia every six to eight weeks. The parents recruited 150 local volunteers to work four shifts a day on the patterning exercises. Billy's older brother and sister also helped.

The parents were pleased with the patterning because Billy "was treated as a person" for the first time, and after awhile, he began to respond. He picked up his head, opened his eyes, and reacted to his environment. The father described the experience as a "challenge." The patterning was continued for several years, until the parents decided that Billy had reached his potential.

They continued to resent their pediatrician's attitude toward Billy and finally found a new doctor, who appeared to take an interest in Billy at first but later treated him more like an animal than a person. The parents finally gave up their quest for a sympathetic doctor and began using the Genetic Counseling Service personnel at a nearby university hospital as their pediatrician.

In the meantime, the couple had another defective son. Once again, doctors tried to get the parents to institutionalize the baby. This time, they went to Philadelphia immediately. However, patterning was not begun, because this child was found to have a heart problem and worse brain damage than Billy.

The wife's mother continued to be supportive, but other family members were not. The family is determined to survive, with or without support from others.

Billy entered a program sponsored by the local association for the retarded, and the mother became involved in the association's mothers' group. She always felt, however, that Billy's problem was far worse than those of the other children.

As Billy has gotten heavier, the parents have had some difficulty finding babysitters for him.

Billy has had major surgery and has had other medical problems. His condition continues to be precarious.[7]

The Crusadership Phase. The parents have accepted the fact that Billy probably will not live much longer. However, they remain active in the association for the retarded. The mother works as a part-time director of volunteers at the association. The parents are also active in the establishment of a peer counseling service for new parents of handicapped children. The mother has spoken about Billy to groups of medical students. She feels that doctors should be better prepared to handle children like Billy. She notes that the medical students have difficulty understanding how she could love such a child.

Although they are afraid to travel far from University Hospital, this family's life is relatively normal in most respects, especially now that their active seekership has ended. Seekership did not stop because solutions were found, however. Rather, the family feels that they have exhausted all possibilities for Billy. Crusadership continues now on a more altruistic level as these parents try to help *future* children like Billy.

CASE 21, 23-25

Background. The father is a 44-year-old maintenance liaison for the board of education, is from a small town in the East, attended but did not graduate from high school, has two siblings. The mother is a 40-year-old housewife, was born in Europe, is a high school graduate, and has three siblings. The family is Catholic. The couple has been married for 21 years. They have five children. The oldest, 21-year-old Joseph, is normal. The remaining children, 19-year-old Tony, 18-year-old Jean, 15-year-old Richard, and 12-year-old Nancy, all have an unusual cerebral palsy-like syndrome, which affects their motor coordination, vision, and learning ability. Jean is confined to a wheelchair. The others are able to walk short distances with crutches. All are legally blind and have been labeled as educable retarded. The family lives in a house owned by the wife's father in an old, but well-kept urban neighborhood in an Eastern metropolis.

The Prenatal Period. Both parents grew up expecting to get married and have children. They knew little about handicaps and expected their children to be normal.

Birth/Postpartum Anomie. All of the children appeared normal at birth. The syndrome had a sudden onset in each case when the child was 5 to 8 months old. With Tony, the parents kept insisting that something was wrong, while their pediatrician kept assuring the mother that he was teething and just neeeded "some tonic to build him up." The baby kept getting worse, and his parents finally took him to the hospital, where his condition was diagnosed as cerebral palsy. The situation was similar in the case of the other three children, although, with each succeeding child, the parents insisted much sooner on hospitalization and diagnosis.

The Plateau Phase. For two and a half years after Tony was diagnosed, nothing was done. During this time, his sister, Jean, was born.

The Seekership Phase. The parents finally called a local

children's hospital because the mother "had always heard it was for crippled children." Tony was admitted there over the objections of the family's pediatrician who said, "You know, Mrs. Jones, he'll never be normal." Tony was an inpatient at the children's hospital for four years.

After Richard was born, the family changed pediatricians because their doctor at first refused to believe that this third child could be handicapped too and later told the children's hospital staff that he had "known it all along." In another "bad experience" with doctors, the parents had taken Nancy to a research hospital in another state, where she was to be admitted as a research patient. When she was discharged, the parents were asked why they bothered bringing her there— she had been an ordinary admission, not a research patient. This turning point prompted the mother to take the initiative to write an eight-page letter of complaint to the administrator of the hospital and to refuse to pay the bill.

At this time, the mother was going to the children's hospital every day. As she said, "I ran myself ragged." Her mother lived upstairs at the time and was very supportive (She has since died). Other family members, however, blamed the parents for having so many handicapped children and were rather hostile toward them.

These parents have been very dissatisfied with their children's education. At the children's hospital, they were in classes with bright children, and "Tony just sat in the corner and played in the sandbox." Later, they went to a school for the blind, which also was not structured for children whose major problem involved a learning disability rather than blindness. Finally, the children entered the public school system, where they were misplaced because no class for the multiply handicapped existed. The school also had no ramps or other accommodations for the handicapped.

Because of their handicaps, these children rarely leave the house alone. In order to improve the quality of their children's lives, the parents have installed a shallow, heated pool in their backyard and have purchased a customized van to transport the children to various events.

Because the mother is often "nervous" about her situation, she has consulted various psychologists, who have blamed her for her problems and not been very helpful.

The parents are currently investigating various sheltered workshop possibilities for their children as they get older.

The Crusadership Phase. This family is an excellent example of *successful* crusadership.

Because no appropriate school program existed for the children, the parents began fighting to *create* one. They wrote letters. The father changed jobs and went to work for the Board of Education. Finally, a program was established, and ramps were installed in the school. The parents are still fighting for better facilities.

In order to improve their children's social life, the parents became active in the local cerebral palsy association. They remain active and are friendly with other parents of handicapped children. They have also established several new activities at the cerebral palsy center, such as a soccer team.

Even this family has established with difficulty a somewhat normalized routine in everyday living. The routine becomes problematic, however, if a "special" outing is planned because of the physical problems involved in manipulating four wheelchairs at once—or—of getting someone to care for the children if the parents want to go out alone.

This family's crusade was not essentially altruistic, because it was undertaken primarily for the family's own children. However, other children with multiple handicaps or cerebral palsy will clearly benefit from the innovations their crusade has accomplished.

Parental careers, then, typically move from anomie to activism in response to a poorly structured society. First, parents seek meaning in their children's conditions, and then, they seek power to control their lives and those of their children. Such seekership is likely to generate conflict between parents and various societal representatives, particularly physicians and school administrators, whose roles have been structured in terms of normality. Finally, some parents move beyond seekership to crusadership in an attempt to change society to meet the needs of those who are different. The difference between seekers and crusaders reflects differences in the opportunity structure rather than any inherent "personality" difference in the parents who follow such paths. Levels of "adjustment," as measured by normalization, then, are directly correlated with favorable structural conditions rather than with the presence or absence of parental pathology. This finding contradicts much of the psychoanalytically oriented literature presented earlier and suggests that *social* change rather than individual therapy might improve the quality of life for these families.

Some of the parents of normal children who were interviewed reported seekership experiences as well. They had been involved in such activities as finding the "right" nursery school for their child, convincing relatives that a baby who seemed "quiet" was perfectly normal, and arguing with a teacher over her evaluation of a child in one area. In no case, however, did these activities become protracted into a career of seekership or crusadership. Rather, they involved isolated incidents in an otherwise "smooth" course of child rearing. Thus, while parental entrepreneurship probably exists in various segments of the population, it reaches its fullest expression as a "way of life" only among those with continuing problems resulting from a child's uncorrectible condition that does not "fit in" with normal social structure.

NOTES

1. Denotes statement made by mother.

2. Denotes statement made by father.

3. All names used in the data presentation are fictitious. However, pseudonyms are used consistently, so that the same pseudonym will always refer to the same child throughout the presentation.

4. A Philadelphia-based program of rigorous stimulation, including "patterned" manipulation of the defective child's body, usually involving large numbers of volunteers.

5. A pediatric nursing instructor of my acquaintance, who has had much experience in hospitals for handicapped children, has told me that this mother's experience is very common in the medical realm as well. Large, poor families are often handed a handicapped child who is discharged from the hospital with a long list of unrealistic instructions for the child's nursing care at home. When these children are later returned to the hospital by parents who say they simply do not have the time or the resources to perform these nursing functions, the parents are seen by medical professionals as irresponsible. She also recalled a case of parents who were chastised after a child's medical apparatus had been jarred loose during the two-day trip in a pickup truck from the child's home to the hospital.

6. One might expect a strong bias in favor of negative responses, given the source of the sample — the files of a genetic counseling service. Parents typically seek genetic counseling *because* they do not want to bring another defective child into the world. Such a motive, however, does not prevent them from loving the defective child they *already have*. Also, as the responses to be presented indicate, a fair number of parents in the sample *would* want another defective child. This latter group may have sought genetic counseling only to increase their knowledge of their child's condition and of their options in family planning, or, simply because their family doctors referred them to the service.

7. Billy died in 1978, after this study was completed.

Chapter 6

THE PEDIATRICIAN'S PERSPECTIVE

As the parents' data indicated, their greatest interactional difficulties involved physicians and other medical personnel. The two areas of greatest conflict were: (1) the situation of first information—most parents were dissatisfied with the manner in which they were told about their children's problems, particularly with the hesitancy of doctors to tell the truth, and (2) the willingness to treat—many parents complained about doctors who did not seem to enjoy treating handicapped children in their everyday practices and who, as a result, treated such children in a less than human manner and treated their parents in a blaming way, especially if they refused institutionalization for their children.

Parents have often been accused in the literature of "projecting" their own guilt onto doctors and other societal representatives. If parents' complaints about physicians were all simply a matter of projection, one might expect that the pediatrician data would reveal: (1) an eagerness to tell the truth in the situation of first information and (2) an eagerness to treat handicapped children in everyday practice. As the following data will reveal, the pediatricians' responses support the parents' view of the situation and do not support the projection hypothesis.

The sample of pediatricians can be characterized as follows: 13 were male, and two were female; all were parents; seven were Protestant, four were Catholic, three were Jewish, and one had no religious affiliation; two had been in practice more than 30 years, 10 had been practicing between 10-and-a-half and 30 years, and three had been in practice for 10 years or less. When asked about the presence of serious birth defects in their own families, eight noted a member with a defect in either their nuclear or extended family, while seven reported no members with a defect.

The pediatricians were asked about how often they were involved in telling parents for the first time that their children had various common birth defects. All of them had informed parents about cerebral palsy, and six of them had done so more than 20 times. All but one had informed parents about Down's Syndrome, about half having done so more than 10 times. All but three had informed parents about neural tube defects; all but four had informed about congenital blindness or deafness. Finally, 10 had informed parents about congenital amputations or serious limb deformities, and seven had informed parents about other syndromes or multiple abnormalities (excluding nonvisible or low-visible defects such as some heart or kidney problems). Thus, all of the pediatricians in the sample had some experience with the situation of first information, and some had a considerable number of such cases.

The Situation of First Information

Almost all of the doctors admitted that they were hesitant to reveal the truth to parents immediately, not because they enjoyed practicing deceit, but because they felt personally uncomfortable with the situation. Most anticipated an emotional reaction from parents that they did not want to face.

Some rationalized their procrastination by arguing that "parents are not ready to hear everything at the beginning."

> Birth is a traumatic experience. For 24 to 48 hours after birth the mother has not returned to a normal psychological state, so I just say everything is O.K., even if it isn't.

> In general, I'm truthful but I don't think you can give them the whole ball of wax right away. You have to allow some time for things to sink in. They don't hear you anyway.

> Mothers are too emotionally wrought up. They don't understand or listen anyway.

> I give them a lot of information on the physical aspects but I hold back on prognosis.

> I don't go through all the possibilities. That's cruel.

> It's not wise to go into all sort of possibilities. I don't want to raise anxiety. Emotionally, they're in shock. They're really not listening.

> I talk about immediate considerations but not long-term complications.

> In general, I lead parents into it gently. I say, "There may be some problem here." I lead them into it. I say, "We're going to take some tests." It depends how sophisticated the person is. In general, I say something is wrong right away but not precisely what it is.

A few doctors said that they had become more truthful over the years, in response to parental demands:

> With my first Down's I kept putting it off. I didn't know how to present it. The parent in that case found it very difficult. . . .Now I tell them right away. One mother has thanked me for telling her right away.

> Initially, I never made a diagnosis of Down's at birth. Everyone told the parents before the doctor did. . . .The parents felt I wasn't interested. One of them came out and said, "You don't care about this baby."

> I tell them right away now because they want to hear.

Several doctors felt they could be more truthful with fathers than with mothers:

> Usually I prefer to tell the father. The mother is in an emotional state after having just given birth.

> Usually I tell the father, and, based on his knowledge of his wife, we decide on a course of action. ...I do this for psychological reasons. My feeling is that you can deal more easily with the father. It's emotionally easier.

> If I had a choice, I'd probably prefer talking to the father first and let him help me make the decision about talking to the mother.

> I call the father and ask him what he wants me to do. I wait until I can reach the father before I talk to the mother.

> I try to talk to the obstetrician to find out if it's the mother's first baby or if she's anxious or apprehensive. ...I always tell the father right away.

In most of these cases, the pediatrician's motivation seems to be based on a sexist notion about the emotional stability of women. All of these doctors were male.[1]

Other pediatricians claimed that they generally told the mother first, out of expediency, because the father was often not present in the hospital and they were too busy to wait for him. Some said that they would later telephone the father in such a case.

Finally, a minority of the pediatricians said they insisted on telling both parents together:

> I feel very strongly that both parents should know what is going on. Daddy is just as interested as mother.

> I don't tell the mother alone. I get them together. There has to be cooperation. ...I wait until they're both together so they can share the burden. Women can usually take it better.

These pediatricians tended to be more truthful and

straightforward in the case of physical defects, particularly correctible ones, than in the case of developmental problems such as cerebral palsy or mental retardation. Many would not talk about a developmental defect until the parents discovered it on their own:

> With cerebral palsy, I sort of lead them into it. I say, "Wait and see." I hedge. Usually I don't call in specialists for two or three months. It depends on parental pressure.

> Very often *they* come in with the question. You can answer questions. . . . The first visit I make a note on the chart. Maybe I make a suggestion to the parent by listening longer to the baby's heart or whatever. By the next visit, parents start to ask. . . . You can't tell them all you know. The specialist can slap them with the facts.

> You suspect this as the child progresses but you don't come right out and say "I think your child has cerebral palsy." You suggest a neurological consultation.

> You start thinking in your mind as you're examining this child month after month. Here you try to hint. You say, "I'm not really sure. We'll watch it a little longer." . . . When you finally tell them they react pretty well.

> I have them come back. I say, "Let's wait."

> If it's something physical, I say I want to get a particular test or study. If it's developmental, I kind of ease them into it. I talk about milestones and what they mean. All along I'm working to get them to realize there's a problem in the child's development. I go slowly. I ask them to come back sooner. . . . I don't seek a consultation right away. Usually the mothers want to see a specialist right away. They want the uncertainty removed.

> There I'll delay. I don't want to worry the parent unnecessarily. I don't use the term, cerebral palsy, very often. The subtle ones, I hedge on. . . . I'm hesitant to come out bluntly and use a term like cerebral palsy. I say, "motor delay" or "developmental lag."

I may sit tight and have them find out. I had one, I knew it was retarded but I wanted (the mother) to see it. ... People are afraid of the word, retardation.

In some cases, the behavior of pediatricians in this situation parallels very closely that of medical personnel in the polio situation discussed by Davis (1960). The prognosis is in fact uncertain in the case of disorders such as Down's Syndrome or cerebral palsy. Such uncertainty makes it easy for doctors to issue no prognosis at all, when in fact, they have *some* idea of what the outcome will be:

> Physical problems are easier to handle. The hardest thing to handle is the uncertainty, which you certainly find in Mongoloids. ... You can't really tell exactly how it's going to be.

> (With Down's Syndrome) I hedge on development. It's variable. You can't be sure.

> Most of the time you can't be sure. Even with Down's, there is such variation.

In such instances, physicians could discuss the *range* of variation but they often say instead, "We can't tell."

The pediatricians were asked if they found some parents more difficult to tell than others. One noted a sexual difference:

> After I've started talking, it's sometimes difficult. I can't stand crying women. There's no sense trying explain any more at that time. Whatever I say, she'll misinterpret.

Others noted an age difference:

> It's much harder with the older mother. She has been waiting for this baby, and the possibility of having more children is not as great.

Older parents don't accept this as well but they're the easiest ones to work with because they have other children. The young parent gets wrought up. ... The young mother doesn't see all the implications.

It's more difficult with immature, emotionally unstable, young couples. Some people don't understand.

Some suggested differences in education and intelligence:

A lot of my telling is the questions they fire at me. The intelligent ones ask a lot of questions.

It depends on their intellectual capacity.

It's easier with parents who are less educated. Others are devastated by a child who carries this label (Down's Syndrome). It's harder to tell the lower class about a major physical deformity. Bright parents do well with physical problems. You choose your words differently for a college graduate and someone with an eighth-grade education. (This physician seems to equate intelligence, education, and social class. Others also made this equation.)

Everything has to be custom-prepared. It depends on the brains of the parent, their sophistication.

Some mentioned differences in emotional stability, and several suggested that such stability was related to ethnic background. Generally, Anglo-Saxons were felt to be easier to tell than "Latins," Italians, or other groups.

The most common factor mentioned by doctors in discussing ease of telling was whether or not they knew the parents prior to the birth:

It's harder if it's people you have known a long time. It's easier to tell people who aren't my own patients in the group.

I may know someone over a period of years. Then I'm the carrier of bad news.

I find it difficult to walk in on a brand new parent, one I've never seen before.

The people hardest to tell are those I don't know. I have to establish a reason for them to trust me.

The pediatricians were asked if they had a general style of telling parents about their children's problems. These were some of their responses:

I try to be as protective of the parent as possible.

I try to sit close to the mother, to be ready for tears.

I say, "I've examined your baby and found everything normal. I do have some concern about the examination of the _____. . . . I don't do this enough. I need to consult a specialist."

I try to be sympathetic and concerned.

I try to be direct but I adapt to circumstances. I'm guided by the husband's feelings.

I start talking about the baby and point out the physical things.

I say, "Everything is generally all right, but we have a problem here."

I give them a general description, then I go into more detail each time I see them.

I'm never satisfied with how I do it. . . . I've taken more time about it now. I've learned that I should present the baby to them or they can't grasp it. I point out the problems by demonstrating the baby to them.

I say, "The baby is basically all right, but it looks like there may be a problem in this area." . . . These (middle class) people ask questions. You don't want to get them too uptight so they can't cope.

Thus, most pediatricians seem to feel they should "break the news gently" and emphasize a child's essential normality.

Such an approach diminishes the likelihood of a difficult emotional confrontation. As one doctor said, "I try to make it as gentle as possible. It's a very hard thing to hear anything about your baby that isn't perfect."

The doctors were asked how *they* felt in the situation of first information, and most replied that they feel uncomfortable and unhappy with their role as "bearers of bad news":

Sad. I'd like everything to be all right. At the beginning I was more personally involved. I've changed with experience...but it still makes me very sad.

I feel sad for the child and the family. When I first started I kind of dreaded it. I wasn't comfortable. ....It doesn't bother me anymore.

I feel very upset.

I feel inadequate.

I feel badly, uncomfortable. I realize the hardship for the family.

It's hard on us because our business is a pleasant business — going into the hospital to see a mother who has just had a baby.

I feel lousy. I hate it. It's the toughest thing in pediatrics.

I don't like it and I don't want to be in that position.

Uncomfortable. It's a very unpleasant thing to have to do.

I don't like it but I accept it. It's the obligation of the physician to comfort the parents as much as possible.

Inadequate. There isn't any way of training people for these things. Some families have a great deal of tragedy, and I feel bad about that. ....I'm sure they don't understand. I'm sure they don't accept, but somebody's got to do it.

I think, "God, this is going to be rough." ...You have intense feelings yourself that you're keeping under control.

Terrible. I was told once that I become too emotionally involved with the patient.

I don't like to have to do it.

Like the parents. I push it away from me.

Thus, the situation of first information is sometimes as hard for the pediatrician as it is for the parents. As a result, doctors try to avoid or postpone the confrontation and then tend to try to ease the parents into the information.

The role of physicians in conveying bad news to the patient's family is in many ways that of the "cooler," described by Goffman (1952): (They must handle) "persons whose expectations and self-conceptions have been built up and then shattered." Goffman notes a number of cooling procedures, however the one typically employed by physicians in the birth defects situation is "stalling":

> When the mark is stalled, he is given a chance to become familiar with the new conception of self he will have to accept before he is absolutely sure that he will have to accept it [Goffman, 1952: 458].

Of course, unlike the professional criminal cooler, pediatricians are in no way responsible for the existence of a child's problem. However, because they have been socialized to cure, physicians feel uncomfortable with the incurable *as though* they had failed in their responsibility to the patient. Stalling, then, enables physicians to, at least temporarily, avoid the uncomfortable situation.

The stalling techniques noted by the pediatricians in this study are of four general types:

(1) *Avoidance.* The physician makes no suggestion at all of the existence of a problem and denies any suggestion by the parent. A variant of avoidance is minimization. Although a defect is noted, its significance is discounted ("He's little...he'll pick up").

(2) *Hinting*. The physician will offer clues by listening longer than usual to the baby's heart or talking about developmental milestones or suggesting diagnostic tests.

(3) *Mystification*. The truth is told in medical jargon or euphemistic terms ("motor delay" or "developmental lag"), so that the parent cannot equate the diagnosis with any known (and presumably dreaded) defect such as cerebral palsy or mental retardation.

(4) *Passing the buck*. The physician refers the parents to a specialist for consultation. Then, the specialist can "slap them with the facts."

These physicians generally rationalize their stalling with the argument that parents are not ready for the truth at the beginning, and most seem to have genuinely convinced themselves that they are acting in the best interest of their patients. However, as the parent data indicated, such stalling almost always increases rather than alleviates parental anxiety.

Willingness to Treat

About half of the doctors said that they did not mind treating children with serious birth defects in their everyday practices, and some even said that they enjoyed such patients:

Sure I see them. I don't treat them any differently. They're the same as the others.

You're always going to have a big spot in your heart for them. . . . Their parents are more cooperative. I've had one or two referred to me who said, "My doctor said this child will never do anything."

When I first went into practice I felt very uneasy about this—you don't get this in residency—but as I had more cases, I learned how to handle it. You treat them normally. I enjoy them about the same as others in my practice. I couldn't work in a mentally retarded home—it would be too depressing—but occasionally, it's a challenge, interesting.

It doesn't bother me. I don't think they have to go to a special doctor. . . . I had a good relationship with one cerebral palsy family in particular.

I treat all kids who come into the office alike. I feel strongly that the youngster with a defect can appreciate the activities in a doctor's office as much as any other kid.

I'm perfectly happy with them. I use specialists but I try to be the one that they relate to. Hospitals try to take over if they have half a chance. That should be what the pediatrician does. I enjoy them just as much as anybody.

My most affectionate patients are Down's patients I've taken care of since birth. In fact, sometimes it's easier. You're more involved with them, you've seen them more, you get to know the parents.

The other pediatricians in the sample, however, candidly admitted that they did not enjoy such patients, and some try to discourage parents from keeping such children at home:

I don't enjoy them. We have several in the practice and we take care of them. I don't see much future for most of them. Some people say that Down's children are very spontaneous, but I don't see the spontaneity — and that's what I enjoy about children.

It's part of the job, but I don't particularly like working with kids who are affected. I worked in a home for the retarded as a student and I got very depressed. I feel adequate to handle the situation but I don't like to. It takes a lot more time.

I only have a couple. I had some that were here and went to other practices nearby. I don't have a particular interest. I'm inadequate and uncomfortable with that sort of problem. I have no special training.

There are personal hang-ups. You go home and see three beautiful, perfect children; then you see this "dud." You can relate more easily to those with three beautiful perfect kids. You can read books, but that's not much help. If somebody comes in with a cerebral palsy or a Down's, I'm not comfortable. ...My inadequacy to the task bothers me. I'm not much help to parents.

I liked problems as a resident but I can't say that I enjoy sick kids anymore. It's hard to find much happiness in this area. The subject of deformed children is depressing. Other problems I can be philosophic about. As far as having a Mongoloid child, I can't come up with anything good it does. There's nothing fun or pleasant. It's somebody's tragedy. I can find good things in practically everything — even dying — but birth defects are roaring tragedies. ...There's nothing interesting about it. ...Death doesn't bother me but the living do. Maybe if I was trained differently I'd have a different outlook.

I don't enjoy it. ...I don't really enjoy a really handicapped child who comes in drooling, can't walk, and so forth. ...Medicine is geared to the perfect human body. Something you can't do anything about challenges the doctor and reminds him of his own inabilities.

I'm not happy. I don't like the fact that they have the problem. It's tough. ...Years ago we could get kids into _____ (State Training Schol) pretty readily. Now they're kept alive.

Personally, I'd like to put every one in an institution. ...I had one case — the grandmother said, "What a cute little thing." I said, "What do you mean? That's a monstrosity." I sent it to a nursery and I didn't send them a bill — a lot of these I've never charged.

I've had a couple of cases — one woman — they went on their own. They got sucked into that quack place down in Philadelphia. They finally came back. ...It was a blessing that this kid died. ...She wanted my notes. I said, "I'll type them for 50 dollars an hour." I said, "The mourning period should be over."

In terms of giving them advice, I've changed in terms of trying to get them to do things that might have seemed "cruel" 20 years ago. Most likely, I recommend institutionalization. I have yet to see a mother who has not been adversely affected by having a Mongoloid child in the house. Despite the fact that women protest and act in a good, competent way, I really feel that it's affected their lives in a way that robs their being a better person. If one is to think that the objective is to make a better life, it interferes with that objective. Seeing these people over the years, . . . the look in their eyes, their demeanor — It's compensatory not fulfilling.

A couple of doctors believed in exerting their professional dominance in situations in which parents must decide on matters such as institutuionalization or whether a child should be treated at all:

It's unfair to expect the parent to make a decision. Very few parents are capable (right after birth). I try to steer them gently in one direction or another. I have a situation now in which the father does not want anything done, and the mother does. In this case, the pediatrician should be steering the mother.

If a child is just a vegetable, I would not do anything heroic to keep it alive. I think it's cruel and barbaric. Mongolianism (sic), spina bifida — should not be kept alive if they have a bad heart. I don't think the mother and father should have a say. I'm very adamant. The doctor should decide. It's tough on the nurses. I have a child in _____ (State Training School) — 40 years old with a mental age of 6 months. I think that's cruel.

I had one baby — retarded. I took the mother by the shoulders and shook her. I told her the baby should die. . . . Later, they thanked me.

This doctor, and others, were rewarded by patients who thanked them. As a result, they felt that their actions were correct. Not one doctor in the sample could recall a single complaint from a parent concerning the doctor's handling of this situation. Such a finding is at first surprising given the widespread dissatisfaction expressed by the parents in this study. Clearly then, parents do not generally express their dissatisfaction directly to doctors, probably because they are intimidated by the physician's professional dominance. Rather, they simply change physicians quietly, and doctors only get feedback from those patients who are satisfied with their treatment. Some doctors do wonder about patients who leave their practice, but as one said,

> It's never come back to me. I have had people who have left and I never heard why, but then, you can't be all things to all people.

Several doctors noted that their abilities in treating handicapped children had been learned through practice, that they had not been adequately trained in medical school to deal with such problems. Indeed, medical students are socialized to make sick people well, and the chronically ill or permanently disabled do not fit such an orientation. Pediatricians are trained to have a bias in favor of basically healthy children.

Traditionally, medical education also locates the source of problems within the individual. Social structure is seen as irrelevant to proper diagnosis and treatment in most cases. Unlike many physically based conditions, however, uncorrectible birth defects are often more of a social then a medical problem. *No matter what* physicians do to their patients, they cannot, within the confines of their role, solve the basic structural problem lodged in the social system. Physicians who cannot change the opportunity structure are likely to feel frustrated, powerless, and inadequate. They suggest institutionalization of those who do not fit in with the system because their training has not shown them how the *system* can be made to fit the individual.

Finally, physicians are, after all, people, and they are affected by the same (usually stigmatizing) socialization toward handicaps as everyone else in society. Interestingly, the physicians' religious backgrounds seemed to have some correlation with their attitudes toward handicapped children: all of the Catholic doctors expressed a willingness to treat, while all of the Jewish doctors (and the one doctor with no religious affiliation) in the sample did not welcome such patients. The attitudes of the Protestant physicians were mixed. Although the sample was not large enough to constitute a truly representative religious cross section, this finding does agree with attitudinal differences reported by Zuk (1959a) in his study of parents. (Ironically, the *parent* data in this study did not reveal any religious difference. Perhaps, parents of all religions learn *of necessity* to accept their children through intensive interaction. Physicians do not share their experiences and are more free to choose the type of patients they prefer. As a result, background factors such as religion may play more of a role in their preferences.) None of the other background factors such as doctor's age or place of medical training seemed to be correlated with attitudes towards handicapped children. However, one doctor in the sample held a view very close to that of the parents and quite unlike that of some of the other physicians. He had had two siblings with myelomeningocele, one who died early and one still alive. He remarked,

> Maybe, there is too much expectation these days that things are to be perfect. ...People have abortions without much thought. ...I'm torn. I have seen my sister grow up with a defect. I have seen people who have learned to accept such things and have a reasonably good life. I think everyone has the right to have their life saved.

Thus, those who have lived with the handicapped,[2] whether they are lay persons or professionals, seem to reject any necessary incompatibility between being handicapped and leading a worthwhile life.

NOTES

1. The male physicians' attitude in these cases may be related to a general view of pregnancy as an illness. Such a view might account for the doctor's paternalistic attitude toward his (female) patient regardless of her sex. Indeed, the female herself has been shown to opt for the sick role during pregnancy in some cases (Rosengren, 1962). However, remarks made by the physicians quoted here at other points in the interview about the "emotional instability" of women suggest that their attitudes have a sexist as well as a paternalistic basis in this situation.

2. This physician was the only one in the sample who had a *nuclear* family member with a *visible*, *disabling* handicap.

Chapter 7

PARENTAL ENTREPRENEURSHIP:
THE MAKING OF A SOCIAL ROLE

In American society, services for the poor, the sick, and the criminal are often predicated on the assumption that the recipients of such services are personally responsible for their condition of need. Ryan (1971) has aptly named this phenomenon, *blaming the victim*. While adults are blamed directly for their problems, parents are typically held responsible for the difficulties of their children. Hence, when students do not do well in ghetto schools, they "are not properly motivated at home," and few suggest that the school might be at fault; juvenile delinquency is attributed to broken homes rather than to an inadquate juvenile justice system, and poor children get sick because their parents do not care for them properly—not because good medical treatment is unavailable to them. Similarly, parents who seek help for their congenitally handicapped children are often defined by professionals in the field as attempting to assuage their own guilt feelings. When such parents disagree with their child's (low-level) school placement, they are "denying the reality" of their child's handicap, and when they object to doctor's orders, they are "projecting their guilt" onto the physician.

This study has explored the relationship between parents' definitions and behavior and those of helping professionals in this area. The preceding chapters have demonstrated how parents of "problem" children can become enmeshed in a movement from apathy to activism as part of a career of entrepreneurship necessitated by a victim-blaming society.

Much of the victim-blaming ideology of professionals in this area derives from the psychoanalytic orientation of literature in the field. As indicated in an earlier chapter, some writers generally assume that parental actions are defense mechanisms aimed at neutralizing the parents' guilt at having given birth to a defective child. As noted earlier, no one is suspicious of a parent who is proud of a normal child, but bragging about the accomplishments of one's handicapped offspring typically becomes defined as denial. Many practitioners have also been trained to approach problems from the perspective of the individual case. As a result, they focus on parental adjustment or acceptance rather than on the structure of the system in looking for solutions.

This ideology apparently forms the basis of much of the treatment that these parents receive from various medical, psychological, educational, and social service practitioners trained in the clinical perspective who work with families of the handicapped. When parents seek help for the various problems their children have, the assumption is made that *something is wrong with the parents*, that they have not reached the stage of mature acceptance (Kanner, 1953) of their child's handicap.

These parents often have difficulty interacting not only with professionals but with lay people as well. Relatives, neighbors, and strangers are likely to be victim-blamers because of the deviant status that such families occupy in a stigmatizing society.

Despite societal stigma, the parents in this study managed to maintain positive definitions of their children. Such definitions did not prevail in the early postpartum period, when most parents still held the stereotyped views of handicaps common to others in society. Eventually, however, these parents undergo a process of resocialization based on their prior socialization in parenthood, intensive interaction with the child, and supportive interaction with others, particularly members of the family and other families with handicapped children (the "own"). This finding is congruent with those of Wortis and Margolies (1955), Voysey (1975), and Hewett (1970), among others. The study findings were very consistent internally as well. The stories of all 40 parents interviewed were strikingly similar, and no major differences were found between mothers and fathers[1] or between parents of younger or older children, even in cases of relatively late diagnosis.[2] Thus, the hypothesized decline in parental acceptance as their children entered adolescence did not materialize among the small number of parents of teenaged children in this study.

Like the members of social movements and deviant subcultures, these parents come to redefine the world, so that the out-group becomes the in-group (See Becker, 1963; Blumer, 1951). Commitment, then, is *strengthened* by adverse reactions from various societal representatives, because these representatives become the "enemy" to the supportive in-group. A child's birth defect cannot be changed; therefore, society must be changed or made responsive to the needs of the child and the child's family. Parents who have been socialized to love, nurture, and socialize their children have no choice but to become entrepreneurs in their own interest. Parental actions can thus be explained as readily in terms of social structure and social interaction as in terms of guilt or defense mechanisms.

Of course, the sample of parents included in the study was "biased" in including only intact families that had chosen to keep their defective children at home. Perhaps those who choose other adaptations differ in their socialization experiences or in the nature and degree of interactional support they receive from significant others. The families in this study managed to cope largely as a result of the strength of the nuclear family and the support of a small number of other members of the in-group. Without this cohesive core of support, the effects of social stigma and victim-blaming might be far more ravaging.

The differing orientations of "deviant" parents and a society structured for those who are "normal" inevitably results in a conflict situation. The first parent-society confrontation occurs shortly after the birth of a defective child, when parents are denied the truth by professionals who are trying to avoid potential conflict and who are in control by virtue of their professional dominance. At the beginning then, parents are likely to be in a state of anomie, with feelings of meaninglessness, resulting from the absence of a truthful diagnosis, and powerlessness, as a result of the professionals' control of the situation.

In an attempt to reestablish the definition of the situation, these parents embark on a career of seekership, somewhat like that of the social movement members described by Lofland and Stark (1965). The first phase of the seekership career involves the procurement of a complete diagnosis. The second phase is directed at finding solutions in the form of responsive medical care, appropriate educational or training programs, and social acceptance. Thus, while the parents of normal children may not have to fight to satisfy their child-rearing needs, the parents in this study were pressed into the role of advocates for their children by a nonresponsive society. Similar advocacy was clearly present in the study of cerebral palsy parents by Hewett (1970) cited earlier. In fact, all of the findings of this study are entirely consistent with hers. Her analysis, however, was different in that she did not analyze her data in interactional or career terms.

The entrepreneurial role develops slowly because of prior socialization in respecting the authority of experts, such as physicians, teachers, and counselors. Hence, most parents initially questioned their doctors' advice or techniques only reluctantly. Doctors are seen and see themselves as authority figures in American society. This authority is often magnified in the case of the male physician and female patient (or mother of a patient) and may produce a relationship of paternalism.

Parents begin to take the initiative in promoting their child's cause as a result of repeated negative interactions with medical, educational, and social agencies, each of which might serve as a critical turning point, combined with support from significant others. Organized associations of parents of children with similar problems play an important role here. As noted earlier, parents often have the courage to "change doctors," for example, after hearing about a successful change made by others. Freidson's (1960) discussion of the lay referral system is very relevant here. As parents become more closely integrated in proparent (and sometimes antiprofessional) networks, their commitment to entrepreneurial activities is likely to increase.

Parental activism probably also received some impetus from the Consumer Movement. After some of the successes of the Civil Rights and Anti-War movements in the 1960s, various oppressed groups in American society began to demand their rights. The Women's Movement and the Consumer Movement no doubt made many individuals in society more aware of the possibility of asserting their interests. Once their consciousness has been raised, parents are probably further inspired by success stories about gains made by the handicap ped that are reported in the media.[3]

Some parents eventually reach a stage of "revelation," in which they discover solutions to most of their children's medical, educational, and social problems. At this turning point, they typically show a marked decline in their entrepreneurial activity—they become less active in parents' associations and they become reintegrated into the routines of normal society. Seekers do not try to change society, but rather, to find a place *within* the existing social structure.

For other parents, especially those whose children have unusual or worsening medical problems, seekership never really ends. Rather, it tends to give way to an elaborated search —crusadership—undertaken by parents in an attempt to establish needed services that do not already exist in society. These parents continue to interact largely within supportive subcultural networks such as parents' assoctions. This mode of action refutes Birenbaum's (1971) theory of the "normal-appearing round of life," because crusaders do not attempt to hide under a guise of normalcy. Birenbaum's interpretation perhaps applies best to the "revealed seeker" who has taken advantage of the solutions offered by society. In those cases in which solutions do not exist, however, parents do not deny the differences between their own and normal families. They may in fact dwell on such differences in their crusades. Revealed seekers may adopt the ideology of rationalization described by Voysey (1975), which emphasizes the similarity between themselves and normals, but this ideology is clearly not universal among parents of handicapped children. Private crusades sometimes become social movements when several parents discover that their problems are shared by others. Crusaders are, thus, reformers, and ultimately perhaps, revolutionaries, in their quest for equal rights with normals.[4]

The various modes of parental action, then, are based on the perceived availability of societal solutions. These modes and various career possibilities are illustrated in Table 8.

Initially in the postpartum period then, parents are somewhat paralyzed by their lack of understanding of their chidren's problems. At this point, they do not love their

TABLE 8: Stages in Careers of Parental Entrepreneurship

TABLE 8: Stages in Careers of Parental Entrepreneurship

Perceived Availability of Solutions by Parents	Mode of Action		
	Apathy/Inertia	Individual Activism	Class Activism

Resignation

Anomie

Private Crusadership

Public Crusadership

Seekership

Normalization

Revelation

Altruism

Parent-Parent Interaction

Parent-Child Interaction

Social Change

Social Change

Social Change

Low

High

children nor are they aware of any societal resources available to help them. Very quickly, however, intensive parent-child interaction results in the development of a significant relationship. Parents' prior socialization in being a good parent and the growth of the parent-child relationship combine to impel the parent to seek help in child rearing from various societal agencies.

In the seekership phase parents become researchers working to discover the solutions that society has to offer. They go to the library, they call other parents of handicapped children, they write letters to national associations for the handicapped. They also ask their doctors, but as one of the pediatricians in the study said, "Parents usually know more than we do about what's available."

Once they begin to get information, parents often also become aware of their relative lack of power, particularly in the medical realm. Especially in cases where children are hospitalized for long periods of time, parents realize that they have very little control over their children's lives. Often when they attempt to gain some measure of control by making demands of medical personnel, they are accused, in victim-blaming fashion, of being meddlesome and uncooperative. Parents persist in their efforts, however, when they discover that some medical treatments (or the lack of treatment when they feel that something should be done) do not work. As Bell (1968) has suggested, parents are likely to engage in more intense parenting with a *nonresponsive* child than a responsive one in an effort to be rewarded. Such intensive parenting is supported by a society that expects parents to "do things" for their children and also by other parents of handicapped children who have successfully gained control over their children's care.

As ordinary means fail to improve a child's condition, parents are likely to seek more extraordinary means such as patterning programs or specialists in other cities. Doctors often refer to such efforts as shopping around for nonexistent cures. As the parents in this study indicated, however, they were not looking for cures as much as for *action*. They felt the need to *do something* for their child. Pediatricians are often unwilling to undertake treatments that do not promise a cure. After all, even if brain-damaged children learn to open their eyes or lift their heads, they will still be profoundly retarded, so "Why bother?" The doctor's orientation is one of treating acute illness, of restoring *normalcy* of function. Correctible physical problems are thus treated with great zeal. Conversely, chronically incapacitating conditions are sometimes not treated at all. (This philosophy reaches its ultimate expression in a case such as spina bifida, when life-saving surgery is deliberately denied the deformed infant). The parental perspective is very different, however. Unlike physicians, parents do not feel that they have failed if their child is not perfectly normal. Success for them involves only "doing the best they can" and achieving a quality of life *as close* to normalcy *as possible*. Thus, while physicians are likely to accuse parents of searching for nonexistent cures, the data of this study indicate that *physicians*, not parents, are sometimes obsessed with cure. Parents are generally willing to settle for treatment that is ameliorative if not curative. A pronouncement that "nothing can be done," then, may not mean to parents that *nothing* can be done.

Hence, parental seekership generally ends when a *close-to-normal* lifestyle has been obtained. Usually, at this point, satisfactory, humane, non victim-blaming medical care has been found in the form of a sympathetic pediatrician, family members are supportive, and children are involved in an educational or training situation where they are learning something. Once such needed services and support have been revealed to parents, normalization is possible.

Although normalization was the most common outcome in such cases, parents do not necessarily have to abandon the subcultural group in favor of normal society. An altruistic adaptation is also possible, as in the case of reformed addicts who devote their time to working with young drug users. Some parents in the sample who had found relatively comfortable adaptations for themselves did choose to volunteer, on a part-time basis, as peer counselors for new parents of handicapped children.

In other cases, seekership ends when all existing possibilities have been exhausted. In this situation, parents can"give up" or resign themselves to the hostilities of a victim-blaming society with the feeling that they did the best they could. Such an outcome is perhaps most likely in the case of a fatal condition, when a child is not expected to live much longer. None of the parents in this study adopted such a resolution, however. Rather, in cases where seekership was unsuccessful, parents continued to fight for their own children or for others.

These unsuccessful seekers, then, became crusaders in an attempt to *create* services for their children: they fought for special classes at school, they established recreational activities for the handicapped, they had ramps built. Such private crusades sometimes become public when, through interaction in parents' associations and in other settings, parents realize that their problems are shared by others. Such group efforts are likely to give rise to social movements, and "antihandicappism" is indeed a growing movement in America today.

Theoretically, crusadership, like seekership, can be successful, if opportunity structures can be changed. When society changes to establish rights for the handicapped equal to those available to normals, crusaders can also achieve normalization (and until society extends those rights to *all* its "deviant" members, crusaders may become altruists in a effort to bring the gains they have achieved to others.)

The process of entrepreneurship is not limited to parents of congenitally handicapped children. The process has always been undertaken to some extent by middle-class parents who seek the best medical care and educational opportunities for their normal children. (Interestingly, the most active crusaders in the group studied here were clearly members of the *working-class*, who had been pushed into activism by a nonresponsive society). Entrepreneurial efforts by parents of normal children are defined in a different way by society, however. If the mother of a normal child becomes upset when her child develops a serious acute illness, her reaction is understandable, and relatives and friends are likely to be sympathetic and supportive. Usually, no ulterior motive is sought for the mother's concern. The classic sick role is, as Freidson (1975) has suggested, only conditionally deviant, and the incumbent is entitled to special considerations and privileges. Those with chronic conditions, however, may be subject to a permanent stigma and may be blamed rather than excused for their failings.

Beyond parents of normal or handicapped children, the theory of entrepreneurship outlined here could be applied to other members of society who seek to change the opportunity structure: minority group members who seek jobs for themselves and others (in this case, powerlessness is probably a larger component of the anomie phase than meaninglessness), consumers who feel oppressed by corporate control of society, and others who become involved in public and private movements of various types. Although the specific dynamics of career movement might be different in each case, the general stages are probably similar. Further research to identify such similarities and differences would be valuable.

This study was not designed to establish generalities that apply to *all*, or even some known proportion of parents of children with birth defects (certainly, further research designed to establish such generalizations would be welcome). Rather, the research was an exploratory attempt, based on samples limited in scope, to *understand* a particular social process involving the interaction between individuals of minority status and the larger society. The parental actions explored here become meaningful when seen in the context of parents' prior socialization experiences, the anomic birth situation, intensive in-group interaction, encouragement from the media, and a society poorly structured to meet the needs of those who are different. Likewise, the actions (and nonactions) of physicians and other professional representatives of society become understandable within a context that establishes a clinical, psychologistic perspective and normalcy as the only criterion of success, reinforcing that criterion through in-group interaction. Differing socialization experiences and needs thus combine to create a conflict situation. A greater awareness on both sides of the sources of difference might help to increase understanding, and possibly, to alleviate some of the conflict, victim-blaming, and hostility that currently prevail.

NOTES

1. Mothers did tend to be somewhat more likely than fathers to be active seekers and crusaders on behalf of their children. This finding is not surprising, given a culturally sanctioned division of labor in which mothers worry about childrearing while fathers worry about career. Interestingly, those fathers in the sample who did play a very active role in seekership/crusadership were from working-class or lower middle-class backgrounds, while those fathers who were least involved tended to be enmeshed in the upper middle-class career drive.

2. The only age-related difference that emerged from the data was that parents of younger children generally found appropriate educational or training programs more quickly than parents whose children were older at the time of the interview. Such a finding is readily explained by social change: More and better programs in special education and infant stimulation are available now, as a result, in some measure, of the efforts of other parents over the years.

3. Numerous examples of parental entrepreneurship can be found in the mass media. One newspaper article reported, for example, that a mother of two spina bifida children who had been "subjected to public insensitivity" speaks before

elementary and high school students using Raggedy Ann and Andy dolls with leg braces to increase children's understanding of the handicapped. Another article has reported on the entrepreneurial activities of the parents of a hearing impaired child in the educational realm:

> The parents told The Press that educating Richie has not been a happy experience for them. Students and teachers haven't always been understanding or helpful, they said. . . .
>
> "At West Woods the teachers care about Richie and treat him like a normal person. Too often his handicap has not been his loss of hearing. . . but the way people treat him," his parents added. . . . The Labutis' are enraged by the treatment given them by some of Richie's teachers. . . . They are perplexed and angry when the microphone, an auditory trainer which helps Richie hear, is not available to him. . . . "Everything Richie has had. . . we have fought for," Mrs. Labutis said in reference to his school needs. . . . Mr. and Mrs. Labutis hope to start a parents' group and meet with the families of other hearing impaired youngsters.
>
> [*The Bristol* (Connecticut) *Press*, May 23, 1977: 5].

Other media examples include a program broadcast by Public Television in 1977 entitled, "Including Me" that documented the successful struggles for education of six handicapped children and their families. Several autobiographical accounts by parents of handicapped children have also appeared in book form. See, for example, *Sticks and Stones* by Elizabeth Pieper and *Bernard: Bringing Up our Mongol Son* by John and Eileen Wilks.

4. Crusadership may take many forms. The author knows of one mother of a spina bifida child (not in the sample) who is currently writing a book entitled, *What to Say After You Say Thank You: Power For Dependent People*. The book is intended to demonstrate the situation of professional dominance and to show patients how to regain control over their medical care.

Although none of the parents in the sample was active in a movement beyond the local level, national organizations of handicapped people, such as the Center on Human Policy and outgrowths of the Center for Independent Living, have been gaining power in recent years.

Chapter 8

TREATMENT WITHOUT CURE?:
SOCIAL PROBLEMS, SOCIAL CHANGE,
AND THE RIGHT-TO-LIFE

This study has suggested that parental entrepreneurs are products of a society that does not provide needed services for certain categories of people. Parents of "problem" children are thus faced with a dilemma: they are socialized by society to feel that good parents help their children grow up in the best possible way but they are denied the tools to implement these teachings. Hence, they become seekers and crusaders in an attempt to *fit*, on the one hand, into the services that society *does* provide, and on the other hand, to *create* the services that society overlooks. In the former case, parents generally adopt the rehabilitation ideology of the helping professionals; in the latter, they opt for the somewhat more radical alternative of restructuring society to meet the needs of individuals.

These conclusions are based on a study of the mothers and fathers of 25 children with serious birth defects living at home in intact families. These parents revealed in depth interviews that they, like other members of society, had hoped that their children would be normal. However, as TST and interview data revealed, they had learned to love the defective children they had, and like other parents, had tried to make their children's lives as fulfilling as possible. By necessity, they adopted a stance of realistic acceptance. Their task was more difficult than that faced by parents of normal children, however, because society is not structured to meet the needs of those who are different. The main focus of the study involved the processes through which these parents coped with, and often overcame, these socially structured barriers.

These parents had difficulty, then, finding physicians who wanted to treat their children and who would treat them humanly. They had difficulty finding school programs that were appropriate for their children's levels of development and learning needs. They had difficulty convincing relatives and neighbors that their children needed love and acceptance just like normal children. They had difficulty finding babysitters who could care for their children while they went shopping or had a chance to relax. They had difficulty paying for expensive equipment their children required and the medical bills that kept accumulating. Finally, they had difficulty finding peace in their lives because the future was more uncertain for them than for parents whose normal children would grow up, leave home, and lead lives of their own.

A small number of parents of normal children were also interviewed. They also expressed concerns relating to the child-rearing process. However, these concerns were not a constant preoccupation for them, as they were for the parents of the handicapped, who often, literally, could not move without taking into account their children's special needs. The group of normal parents who were interviewed was not large enough by any means to constitute a control group for the study. Further research is indicated here to show just *how different* these parents' lives are from those of people whose children are normal.

A sample of 15 pediatricians was also interviewed to obtain a greater understanding of the views of one societal agency with which parents must frequently interact. Some doctors were quite sympathetic toward parents of handicapped children. Others were not. A few were decidedly hostile toward parents who kept such children at home. These doctors' views are understandable within the context of their socialization in a stigmatizing society and their training in medical school, where success is typically equated with curing and normalcy of function and problems are treated on an individualistic rather than a societal basis.

This study did not measure the self-concepts of the children whose families were involved. Indeed, some may have lacked the mental development necessary for self-concept formation. Most, however, appeared to be happy and were believed to be content by their parents. Certainly, to the extent that parental attitudes influence children's self-esteem, these children are likely to see themselves somewhat favorably. All of the parents would probably agree too, that although their children's lives were not perhaps of the highest quality, they all derived some enjoyment and satisfaction out of living. Many parents were also careful to point out that *they* had benefited from their children's lives, through increased awareness, compassion, understanding, and tolerance, that they had become "better people." Thus, while some parents would not have wanted their children to have been born, all felt that once born, their children's lives had some value.

Others in society did not always recognize that value, however, forcing parents to fight for their children's rights. Prior to the birth of their children, most of these parents shared the stereotyped and stigmatizing conceptions of handicaps held by the rest of society. Once their children were born, parents learned through intensive interaction that, like normal children, their offspring were human and lovable.

While they were not happy with their children's defects, they were realistically accepting of them. Others in society who did not share their intensive interaction experiences continued of course to stereotype and stigmatize, driving parents into the entrepreneurial role.

These findings have relevance for a greater understanding of a variety of social problems. Responses that are defined as pathological in the professional ideology of service agencies may in fact be realistic adaptations to difficult situations that are only understandable within the interactional context of those situations. Individuals and families seem to be quite flexible in adapting to stress, yet the normative definitions by which they are judged are much more unbending. Thus, those with problems are forced into resourcefulness to meet the demands of society.

Medical ethics is always concerned with the question of whether the severely handicapped have a right to life. In many cases, deformed babies are denied medical treatment, because doctors feel that their lives would be filled with problems. Physicians are often reinforced in this view by the feeling that parents concur in their definition of the situation. Lorber (1973) comments, for example, that most parents of newborns with spina bifida accept his criteria as a basis for refusing treatment to their babies. However, parents are probably highly suggestible in this situation and likely to accept a clear-cut alternative presented by an authority figure—the physician. Also, as the data of this study have indicated, parents are anomic and do not yet love their children at this point. The negative reactions to severely handicapped children expressed by some of the physicians interviewed in this study conform with medical judgments to withhold necessary treatment from these children as newborns. These doctors are socialized to have a bias in favor of perfect mental and physical health, to be rewarded by curing the sick and making them well. When curing is not possible, treating is sometimes abandoned as well.

Certainly, given the present structure of a society poorly designed to accommodate individual differences, the assessment of these doctors, with respect to the future of such children, is accurate; their lives *are* likely to be filled with problems. However, perhaps the issue should be more complex. As the findings of this study have indicated, a life defined by physicians as intolerable might come to be defined in a very different manner by parents. The perspective of the sociology of knowledge makes such differences in values understandable. As this study has indicated, the social worlds of parents and physicians vary considerably.

These findings have relevance for the current controversy over the treatment of infants born with myelomeningocele-hydrocephalus. The popular treatment policy in Britain and the United States noted earlier, based on criteria established by Lorber (1971), is derived from a medically based world view that equates quality of life with complete normalcy of function. As this study has shown, parents' definitions of their children are likely to include a variety of expressive and instrumental traits in addition to physical and mental normalcy. These definitions are, further, interactional in nature and subject to change over time, and hence, not totally predictable at birth. As the author has noted elsewhere (Darling, 1977, 1978), those charged with deciding whether these infants should live or die ought to be aware of the *possibility* of positive outcomes such as some of those described in this study as well as of the values involved in constructing any treatment policy.

One might still argue that no matter how accepting parents learn to be, their quality of life and that of their children will be marred by the lack of acceptance by the rest of society. Indeed, this study has demonstrated that the problems encountered by these parents in everyday social interaction can be enormous, and many would not have wanted their children to be born given current social structure and values. However, if society were restructured to fit the needs of various "deviant" groups through the provision of appropriate services, the problems of these groups would be greatly reduced. Such a change in society would be contingent on some important, and perhaps unlikely, changes in values. Yet, as a pediatrician quoted earlier said, "Maybe there is too much expectation these days that things are to be perfect." Social problems are not problems unless they are defined as such by those who have power in society. A greater tolerance and provision for pluralism rather than perfection might make us all, in the words of a number of parents quoted earlier, "better people."

APPENDICES

APPENDIX A

INTERVIEW FORM

Child's Name _____ M   F

D.O.B. _____ Nature of Problem_____

Father's Name_____ Mother's Name_____
(Circle interviewee)

Age _____   _____
Race _____   _____
Original
Nationality _____   _____
Birthplace _____   _____
Occupation _____   _____
Religion _____   _____
Education
(completed) grade school ____   _____
            high school _____   _____
            college _____   _____
            grad school _____   _____
Size of
family of
origin _____   _____
First
marriage? _____   _____
Date of present marriage _____

Do you have any children beside _____?

Name	Age	Any birth defects or serious medical problems?
_____	____	_____
_____	____	_____

PRENATAL

First, I'd like to talk about the time before _____ was born.
Have you always wanted children? Why?
Did you have much experience with children be-
fore _____ was born?
(If not the first) Why did you want *this* child?
Did you know anything about _____ (defect) be-
fore _____ was born?
How did you feel about handicapped children at that time?
What was the pregnancy like?
Do you remember some of the things you were thinking right be-
fore _____ was born?
Who were the people who were important to you at that time?
What were their attitudes toward your pregnancy? Did they have
any preferences with respect to your child (sex, etc.)? How did their
feelings affect you?
What was happening in your family at the time of the birth?

BIRTH

Were you awake (present) for the birth? Can you describe what
happened in the delivery room? How was it the same as (different
from) what you expected? Did you suspect (know) that something
was wrong with your child at that time?
If you were not awake (present) for the birth, how did you learn
about the problem? Did you understand the first explanation you
received? What was your reaction? What was the reaction of your
spouse, doctor, hospital personnel, family, friends? What sorts of
things did you think about at the time?
When did you see the baby for the first time? How did you feel
about _____ (child's name) then?
What were your expectations for your baby's future at that time?

POSTPARTUM

(If child's problem was not apparent at birth: Did it become
known to you before you/your wife left the hospital? How?—
describe in detail.)

Did you see (handle) the baby before you left the hospital?—note extent of early contact.

Did the baby leave the hospital with you (your wife)? How did you feel about him (her) then? What were your major concerns at that time?

How did your other children, friends, neighbors, relatives, coworkers, social worker, clergyman, visiting nurse, etc. react to _____ when he (she) first came home? Who were the people you saw the most at that time? How did their reactions affect you?

Did you ever consider institutionalization or foster care at that time?

INFANCY

(If child's problem was not apparent during hospital stay: When did you suspect or find out that something was wrong?—document)—Immediate reaction. Did you accept the first diagnosis?

Did you have any difficulty caring for the baby at home?

What kind of baby was he (she)? Was he (she) different from what you expected?

Did you spend a lot of time with him (her)? How did your spouse, other children feel about that? How did their reactions affect you?

Who were the people, outside your immediate family, who were closest to you at the time? How did they react to the baby? How did that affect you? Did anyone react negatively to the baby? Have you lost any friends because of _____ ?

When did you take the baby out of the house for the first time? How did strangers react? How did their reactions affect you? Did you take the baby out as often as you had your other children?

Did you talk to any other parents of a child with _____ ? Did you join any organized groups?

Was _____ hospitalized at all during his (her) first year of life? Elaborate. How were you affected by the experience?

What about clinic visits, checkups, etc.—what was your experience with doctors, nurses, therapists, etc.? Other parents and their children?

How did your relationship with the baby develop during the first year? How did this compare with what you expected?

Did you ever consider institutionalization or foster care?

What other kinds of things were going on in your life at the time?

EARLY CHILDHOOD

How did your child's development progress—socially, physically (appearance, toilet training, feeding, health, motor development, etc.), intellectually? Are these areas of development important to you? How have other people evaluated your child's performance in these areas? Is this important to you?

Did _____ attend nursery school or any type of preschool program? How did he (she) do there?

Any hospitalizations during preschool years?—effect on child and family.

Did your child have a chance to play with other children his (her) age at that time? Did he (she) get along well with them? How did you feel about this?

Any therapy programs? Performance? Evaluation by doctors, nurses, therapists, others?

Who were the people most important to you at that time (those to whom you referred yourself when confronted with a problem)?

How did your family and friends feel about _____ at this time? What kinds of problems arose?

Reactions of strangers? How did this affect you?

LATER CHILDHOOD

Who are the people who are most important to you at the present time? How do these people feel about _____? How do you feel about that?

Does your child attend school? How is he (she) doing there? How do his (her) teachers feel about him (her)?

Does your child have friends? Handicapped? Normal? How does he (she) get along with them? How do you feel about this?

Does your child participate in any extra-curricular activities, hobbies, lessons, etc.? Is this important to you?

Any recent hospitalizations, therapy programs, etc.? Effect on child and family.

How do you think strangers feel when they meet _____ for the first time? How does this affect you?

TO BE ASKED AT END OF INTERVIEW:

How do you feel about_____'s development so far? In what areas would you like to see improvement? How do you feel about _____ as a person? Do you wish he (she) were different in any way?

What is your relationship with _____ like? How much time do you spend with him (her)?

Do you feel that your life is limited in any way by having at home? Does this bother you?

What other kinds of things are going on in your life now?

What are your expectations for _____'s future?

Would you have another child like   ?

If you had had some way of knowing, before _____ was *conceived* that he/she would have this problem, would you have wanted him/her to be born?

APPENDIX B

PEDIATRICIANS' INTERVIEW

Date
Name
Address
Phone

Sex _____   Birthplace _____
Race _____   Marital Status_____
Age _____   Children? ages _____
Original nationality _____
Religion _____
Length of practice _____
Where did you receive your medical training?

Is there anyone in your own family with a serious birth defect?

Each year in your practice, about how often would you say you are involved in telling parents for the first time that their child has any of the following birth defects (excluding stillborns):

Down's Syndrome   _____

Neural tube defects   _____

Congenital blindness   _____

or deafness   _____

CP   _____

Congenital amputation
or serious limb
deformities   _____

Other syndromes or multiple
congenital abnormalities_____
Which ones?_____

1. In the case of defects apparent at birth or shortly thereafter, such as myelomeningocele or Down's Syndrome, do you usually tell parents right away or do you wait? Why?

2. Do you prefer to tell the mother or father first, or do you wait until you can tell them both together? Why?

3. How much do you usually tell them at the beginning? Do you ever hold back any information? Why?

4. Do you find it more difficult to tell some parents than others? Do you tell everyone the same way, or, change the explanation for different cases?

5. Do you handle different defects differently?

6. Do you feel that it is important to present an optimistic picture to parents at the beginning, or is it better to make them aware of all of the worst possibilities right away so they will be prepared?

7. Would you say that you have a general "style" or way of telling parents about their babies' problems? Have you always done it this way? If not, how and why have you changed?

8. How do parents usually react in this situation? Do mothers and fathers react differently? Older parents versus younger? Those with various social backgrounds? How do you think they feel?

9. What kinds of questions do parents usually ask? Do you think that most parents are satisfied with your explanation?

10. How do *you* feel in this situation? Have you ever felt that you didn't handle it the right way? Has a parent ever complained to you about your handling of the situation?

11. In the case of defects that don't become apparent until sometime after birth, such as cerebral palsy or congenital blindness, how do you handle telling the parents? (Repeat question 3-10.)

12. How do you feel about treating children with serious birth defects such as Down's Syndrome in your everyday practice? Do you ever feel uneasy about relating to them?

REFERENCES

BACKMAN, C. W. (1963) "Resistance to change in self-concept as a function of consensus among significant others." Sociometry 26 (March): 108.

BARSCH, R. H. (1961) "Explanations offered by parents and siblings of brain-damaged children." Exceptional Children 27 (January): 286-291.

BAUM, M. H. (1962) "Some dynamic factors affecting family adjustment to the handicapped child." Exceptional Children 28: 387-392.

BECKER, H. S. (1970) "Whose side are we on?" pp. 15-25 in W. J. Filstead (ed.) Qualitative Methodology: Firsthand Involvement With the Social World. Chicago: Markham.

—— (1963) Outsiders: Studies in the Sociology of Deviance. New York: The Free Press.

BEHRENS, M. L. (1954) "Child rearing and the character structure of the mother." Child Development 25: 225-238.

BELL, R. L. (1968) "A reinterpretation of the direction of effects in studies of socialization." Psychological Review 75 (March): 81-95.

BERNABEU, E. P. (1958) "The effects of severe crippling on the development of a group of children." Psychiatry 21: 169-194.

BIRENBAUM, A. (1971) "The mentally retarded child in the home and the family cycle." Journal of Health and Social Behavior 12 (March): 55-65.

—— (1970) "On managing a courtesy stigma." Journal of Health and Social Behavior 11 (September): 196-206.

BLUM, F. H. (1970) "Getting individuals to give information to the outsider," pp. 83-90 in W. J. Filstead (ed.) Qualitative Methodology: Firsthand Involvement With the Social World. Chicago: Markham.

BLUMER, H. (1969) Symbolic Interactionism: Perspective and Method. Englewood Cliffs, NJ: Prentice-Hall.

—— (1951) "Social movements," pp. 199-219 in A. M. Lee (ed.) Principles of Sociology. New York: Barnes and Noble.

BOLES, G. (1959) "Personality factors in mothers of cerebral palsied children." Genetic Psychology Monographs 59 (May): 160-218.

CALDWELL, B. M. and S. B. GUZE (1960) "A study of the adjustment of parents and siblings of institutionalized and noninstitutionalized retarded children." American Journal of Mental Deficiency 64 (March): 845-861.

CENTERS, L. and R. CENTERS (1963) "A comparison of the body image of amputee and nonamputee children as revealed in figure drawings." Journal of Projective Techniques and Personality Assessment 27 (June): 158-165.

COLLINS, H., G. K. BURGER, and D. DOHERTY (1970) "Self-concept of EMR and nonretarded adolescents." American Journal of Mental Deficiency 75: 285-289.

COOLEY, C. H. (1964) Human Nature and the Social Order. New York: Schocken.

COOPERSMITH, S. (1967) The Antecedents of Self-Esteem. San Francisco: W. H. Freeman.

COUCH, C. J. and J. S. MURRAY (1964) "Significant others and evaluation." Sociometry 27 (December): 502-509.

CRUICKSHANK, W. M. and J. MEDVE (1948) "Social relationships of physically handicapped children." Journal of Exceptional Children 14: 100-106.

CUMMINGS, S. T. (1966) "Effects of the child's deficiency on the mother: a study of mothers of mentally retarded, chronically ill, and neurotic children." American Journal of Orthopsychiatry 36 (July): 595-608.

D'ARCY, E. (1968) "Congenital defects: mothers' reactions to first information." British Medical Journal 3 (September): 796-798.

DARLING, R. B. (1978) "Reply to Lowell E. Sever." Hastings Center Report 8 (February): 4, 43.

—— (1977) "Parents, physicians, and spina bifida: a study of values in conflict." Hastings Center Report 7 (August): 10-14.

DAVIS, F. (1961) "Deviance disavowal: the management of strained interaction by the visibly handicapped." Social Problems 9: 120-132.

—— (1960) "Uncertainty in medical prognosis clinical and functional." American Journal of Sociology 66 (July): 41-47.

—— (1956) "Definitions of time and recovery in paralytic polio convalescence." American Journal of Sociology 61: 582-587.

DENHOFF, E. and R. H. HOLDEN (1971) "Understanding parents: one need in cerebral palsy," pp. 255-263 in R. L. Noland (ed.) Counseling Parents of the Ill and the Handicapped. Springfield, Il: Charles C. Thomas.

—— (1954) "Family influence on successful school adjustment of cerebral palsied children." Exceptional Children 21 (October): 5-7.

DORNER, S. (1975) "The relationship of physical handicap to stress in families with an adolescent with spina bifida." Developmental Medicine and Child Neurology 17: 765-776.

DOW, T. E., Jr. (1966) "Optimism, physique and social class in reaction to disability." Journal of Health and Social Behavior 7 (Spring): 14-19.

DOWNEY, K. J. (1963) "Parental interest in the institutionalized severely mentally retarded child." Social Problems 11 (Fall): 186-193.

DUFF, R. S. and A. G. M. CAMPBELL (1973) "Moral and ethical dilemmas in the special-care nursery." The New England Journal of Medicine 289 (October 25): 890-894.

EISENSTADT, A. A. (1971) "Psychological problems of the parents of a blind child," pp. 377-384 in R. L. Noland (ed.) Counseling Parents of the Ill and Handicapped. Springfield, Il: Charles C. Thomas.

ELKIN, F. (1960) The Child and Society. New York: Random House.

FARBER, B. (1960) "Perceptions of crisis and related variables in the impact of a retarded child on the mother." Journal of Health and Human Behavior 1 (Summer): 108-118.

FLAPAN, D. (1968) Children's Understanding of Scoial Interaction. New York: Columbia University Teachers' College Press.

FORD, A. B. (1967) The Doctor's Perspective: Physicians View Their Patients and Practice. Cleveland, OH: The Press of Case Westen Reserve University.

FORRER, G. R. (1959) "The mother of a defective child." Psychoanalytic Quarterly 28: 59-63.

FOWLE, C. M. (1968) "The effect of the severely mentally retarded child on the family." American Journal of Mental Deficiency 73 (November): 468-473.

FREEMAN, H. E. and O. G. SIMMONS (1961) "Feelings of stigma among relatives of former mental patients." Social Problems 8: 312-321.

—— (1959) "Social class and posthospital performance levels." American Sociological Review 2 (June): 348.

FREEMAN, J. M. [ed.] (1974) Practical Management of Meningomyelocele. Baltimore, MD: University Park Press.

FREESTON, B. M. (1971) "An inquiry into the effect of a spina bifida child upon family life." Developmental Medicine and Child Neurology 13: 456-461.

FREIDSON, E. (1975) Profession of Medicine. New York: Dodd Mead.

—— (1970) Professional Dominance. Chicago: Aldine.

—— (1961) Patients' Views of Medical Practice. New York: Russell Sage Foundation.

FRIEDMAN, S. B. (1963) "Behavioral observations of parents anticipating the death of a child." Pediatrics 32 (October): 610-625.

GLASER, B. G. and A. L. STRAUSS (1965) Awareness of Dying. Chicago: Aldine.

—— (1964) "Awareness contexts and social interaction." American Sociological Review 29 (October): 669-679.

GOFFMAN, E. (1963) Stigma: Notes on the Management of Spoiled Identity. Englewood Cliffs, NJ: Prentice-Hall.

—— (1952) "On cooling the mark out: some aspects of adaptation to failure." Psychiatry 15 (November): 451-463.

GOLDY, F. B. and A. H. KATZ (1971) "Social adaptation in hemophilia," pp. 432-442 in R. L. Noland (ed.) Counseling Parents of the Ill and Handicapped. Springfield, IL: Charles C. Thomas.

GOODMAN, N., S. M. DORNBUSCH, S. A. RICHARDSON, and A. H. HASTORF (1963) "Variant reactions to physical disabilities." American Sociological Review 28: 429-435.

GOODSTEIN, L. D. (1960) "MMPI differences between parents of children with cleft palates and parents of physically normal children." Journal of Speech and Hearing Research 3 (March): 31-38.

GREBLER, A. M. (1952) "Parental attitudes toward mentally retarded children." American Journal of Mental Deficiency 56 (January): 475-483.

GREEN, M. and A. J. SOLNIT (1964) "Reactions to the threatened loss of a child: a vulnerable child syndrome." Pediatrics 34 (July): 58-66.

HARE, E. H. (1966) "Spina bifida cystica and family stress." British Medical Journal 2 (September): 757-760.

HAUG, M. R. and M. B. SUSSMAN (1969) "Professional autonomy and the revolt of the client." Social Problems 17 (Fall): 153-161.

HAVIGHURST, R. J. and A. DAVIS (1955) "A comparison of the Chicago and Harvard studies of social class differences in child rearing." American Sociological Review 20: 438-442.

HAWKES, G. R. (1956) "Parents' acceptance of their children." Journal of Home Economics 48: 195-200.

HEILMAN, A. E. (1950) "Parental adjustment to the dull handicapped child." American Journal of Mental Deficiency 54 (April) 556-562.

HELPER, M. M. (1958) "Parental evaluations of children and children's self-evaluations." Journal of Abnormal and Social Psychology 56 (March): 190-194.

HEWETT, S. (1970) The Family and The Handicapped Child: A Study of Cerebral Palsied Children in Their Homes. Chicago: Aldine.

HOLT, K. S. (1958) "The home care of severely retarded children." Pediatrics 22 (September): 744-755.

HORROBIN, J. M. and J. E. RYNDERS (n.d.) To Give an Edge: A Guide For New Parents of Down's Syndrome (Mongoloid) Children. Minneapolis, MN: Colwell.

HYMAN, H. (1942) "The psychology of status." Archives of Psychology 269.

HYMAN, H. H., J. STOKES and H. M. STRAUSS (1973) "Occupational aspirations among the totally blind." Social Forces 51 (June): 403-416.

JAMES, W. (1890) The Principles of Psychology. New York: Holt.

JENNINGS, H. H. (1950) Leadership and Isolation. New York:

JONES, S. C. (1968) "Some effects of interpersonal evaluations on group process and social perception." Sociometry 31 (June): 150-161.

JORDAN, T. E. (1971) "Physical disability in children and family adjustment," pp. 10-26 in R. L. Noland (ed.) Counseling Parents of the Ill and Handicapped. Springfield, IL: Charles C. Thomas.

—— (1962) "Research on the handicapped child and the family." Merrill-Palmer Quarterly 8: 243-260.

JOURARD, S. M. and R. M. REMY (1955) "Perceived parental attitudes, the self and security." Journal of Consulting Psychology 19 (October): 364-366.

KANNER, L. (1953) "Parents' feelings about retarded children." American Journal of Mental Deficiency 57 (January): 375-383.

KELLEY, H. H. (1952) "Two functions of reference groups," pp. 410-414 in G. E. Swanson et al. (eds.) Readings in Social Psychology. New York: Holt.

KEMPER, T. D. (1966) "Self conceptions and the expectations of others." Sociological Quarterly 7 (Summer): 323-343.

KINCH, J. W. (1968) "Experiments on factors related to self-concept change." Journal of Social Psychology 74: 251-258.

—— (1963) "A formalized theory of the self-concept." American Journal of Sociology 68 (January): 481-486.

KALUS, M. H. (1972) "Maternal attachment: importance of the first post-partum days." New England Journal of Medicine 286 (March): 460-463.

KLECK, R., H. ONO and A. H. HASTORF (1966) "The effects of physical deviance upon face-to-face interaction." Human Relations 19 (November): 425-436.

KOHN, M. L. (1963) "Social class and parent-child relationships: an interpretation." American Journal of Sociology 68 (January): 471-480.

—— (1959) "Social class and parental values." American Journal of Sociology 64 (January): 337-351.

KOLIN, I. S. (1971) "Studies of the school-age child with meningomyelocele: social and emotional adaptation." Journal of Pediatrics 78 (June): 1013-1019.

KRIDER, M. A. (1959) "A comparative study of the self-concepts of crippled and non-crippled children." Dissertation Abstracts 20: 4-6: 2143.

KUHN, M. (1967) "The reference group reconsidered," pp. 171-184 in J. G. Manis and B. N. Meltzer (eds.) Symbolic Interaction. Boston: Allyn & Bacon.

—— (1962) "The interview and the professional relationship," pp. 193-206 in A. Rose (ed.) Human Behavior and Social Processes. Boston, MA: Houghton Mifflin.

—— and T. S. McPARTLAND (1954) "An empirical investigation of self-attitudes." American Sociological Review 19 (February): 68-76.

LEMERT, E. M. (1967) Human Deviance, Social Problems, and Social Control. Englewood Cliffs, NJ: Prentice-Hall.

—— (1951) Social Pathology. New York: McGraw-Hill.

LITMAN, T. (1962) "Self-conception and physical rehabilitation," pp. 537-574 in A. M. Rose (ed.) Human Behavior and Social Processes. Boston, MA: Houghton Mifflin.

LOFLAND, J. and R. STARK (1965) "Becoming a world saver: a theory of conversion to a deviant perspective." American Sociological Review 30 (December): 862-875.

LORBER, J. (1973) "Early results of selective treatment of spina bifida cystica." British Medical Journal 4: 201-204.

——— (1971) "Results of treatment of myelomeningocele." Developmental Medicine and Child Neurology 13: 279-303.

MANDELBAUM, A. and M. E. WHEELER (1960) "The meaning of a defective child to parents." Social Casework 41 (July): 360-367.

MARTIN, P. (1975) "Marital breakdown in families of patients with spina bifida cystica" Developmental Medicine and Child Neurology 17: 757-764.

MATZA, D. (1964) Delinquency and Drift. New York: John Wiley.

MAWARDI, B. H. (1965) "A career study of physicians." The Journal of Medical Education 40 (July): 658-666.

MAYER, C. L. (1967) "Relationships of self-concepts and social variables in retarded children." American Journal of Mental Deficiency 72: 267-271.

MCCOLLUM, A. T. and L. E. GIBSON (1970) "Family adaptation to the child with cystic fibrosis." Journal of Pediatrics 77 (October): 571-578.

MCDONALD, E. L. (1971) "Understand those feelings," pp. 44-51 in R. L. Noland (ed.) Counseling Parents of the Ill and the Handicapped. Springfield, IL: Charles C. Thomas.

MCHUGH, P. (1968) Defining the Situation. Indianapolis, IN: Bobbs-Merrill.

MEAD, G. H. (1934) Mind, Self and Society. Chicago: University of Chicago Press.

MEADOW, K. P. (1968) "Parental response to the medical ambiguities of congenital deafness." Journal of Health and Social Behavior 9 (December): 299-309.

MEDINNUS, G. R. and F. J. CURTIS (1963) "The relation between maternal self-acceptance and child acceptance." Journal of Consulting Psychology 27 (December): 542-544.

MEISSNER, A. L., R. W. THORESON, and A. J. BUTLER (1967) "Relation of self-concept to impact and obviousness of disability among male and female adolescents." Perceptual and Motor Skills 24: 1099-1105.

MERCER, J. R. (1965) "Social system perspective and clinical perspective: frames of reference for understanding career patterns of persons labeled as mentally retarded." Social Problems 13 (Summer): 18-34.

MERTON, R. K. and A. S. ROSSI (1957) "Contributions to the theory of reference group behavior," pp. 225-280 in R. K. Merton, Social Theory and Social Structure. New York: Free Press.

MESSINGER, S. L. (1962) "Life as theater: some notes on the dramaturgic approach to social reality." Sociometry 25: 98-110.

MEYEROWITZ, J. H. (1962) "Self-derogations in young retardates and special class placement." Child Development 33: 443-451.

——— and H. B. KAPLAN (1967) "Familial responses to stress: the case of cystic fibrosis." Social Science and Medicine 1 (September): 249-266.

MILLER, L. G. (1968) "Toward a greater understanding of the parents of the mentally retarded child." Journal of Pediatrics 73: 699-705.

MIYAMOTO, S. F. and S. M. DORNBUSCH (1956) "A test of interactionaist hypotheses of self-conception." American Journal of Sociology 61 (March): 399-403.

PIEPER, E. (1977) Sticks and Stones. Syracuse, N.Y.: Human Policy Press.

PIERS, E. V. (1972) "Parent prediction of children's self-concepts." Journal of Consulting and Clinical Psychology 38: 428-433.

PORTER, B. M. (1954) "Measurement of parental acceptance of children." Journal of Home Economics 46: 176-182.

POWELL, F. D. (1975) Theory of Coping Systems: Changes in Supportive Health Organizations. Cambridge, MA: Schenkman.

QUARANTELLI, E. J. and J. COOPER (1966) "Self-conceptions and others: a further test of Meadian hypotheses." Sociological Quarterly 7 (Summer): 281-297.

QUINT, J. C. (1965) "Institutionalized practices of information control." Psychiatry 28 (May): 119-132.

RAINWATER, L. (1966) "Crucible of identity." Daedalus (Winter): 160-204.

RAY, M. B. (1964) "The cycle of abstinence and relapse among heroin addicts," pp. 163-177 in H. S. Becker (ed.) The Other Side. New York: Free Press.

REID, E. S. (1971) "Helping parents of handicapped children," pp. 52-61 in R. L. Noland (ed.), Counseling Parents of the Ill and the Handicapped. Springfield, IL:. Charles C. Thomas.

RICHARDSON, S. A. (1971) "Children's values and friendships: a study of physical disability." Journal of Health and Social Behavior 12 (September): 253-258.

——— (1970) "Age and sex differences in values toward physical handicaps." Journal of Health and Social Behavior 11 (September): 207-214.

——— (1969) "The effect of physical disability on the socialization of a child," pp. 1047-1064 in D. A. Goslin (ed.) Handbook of Socialization Theory and Research. Chicago: Rand McNally.

———, N. GOODMAN, A. H. HASTORF, and S. M. DORNBUSCH (1961) "Cultural uniformity in reaction to physical disabilities." American Sociological Review 26 (April): 241-247.

———, A. H. HASTORF, and S. M. DORNBUSCH (1964) "Effects of physical disability on a child's description of himself." Child Development 35 (September): 893-907.

ROBINSON, W. S. (1951) "The logical structure of analytic induction." American Sociological Review 16 (December):

ROSEN, G. M. and A. O. ROSS (1968) "Relationship of body image to self-concept." Journal of Consulting and Clinical Psychology 32: 100.

ROSENBERG, M. (1965) Society and the Adolescent Self-Image. Princeton, NJ: Princeton Unversity Press.

——— (1963) "Parental interest and children's self-conceptions. Sociometry 26 (March): 35-49.

——— and R. G. SIMMONS (1971) Black and White Self-Esteem: The Urban School Child. Washington, DC: American Sociological Association.

ROSENGREN, W. R. (1962) "The sick role during pregnancy: a note on research in progress." Journal of Health and Human Behavior 3: 213-218.

ROTH, J. A. (1962) "The treatment of tuberculosis as a bargaining process," pp. 575-588 in A. Rose (ed.) Human Behavior and Social Processes. Boston, MA: Houghton Mifflin.

RYAN, W. (1971) Blaming the Victim. New York: Random House.

SALK, L. (1972) "The psychosocial impact of hemophilia on the patient and his family." Social Science and Medicine 6: 491-505.

SCHECHTER, M. D. (1961) "The orthopedically handicapped child: emotional reactions." Archives of Genral Psychology 4: 247-253.

SCHEFF, T. J. (1966) Being Mentally Ill: A Sociological Theory. Chicago: Aldine.

SCHIPPER, M. T. (1959) "The child with mongolism in the home." Pediatrics 24 (July): 132-144.

SCHONELL, F. J. and M. RORKE (1960) "A second survey of the effects of a subnormal child on the family unit." American Journal of Mental Deficiency 64 (March): 862-868.

——— and B. H. WATTS (1956) "A first survey of the effects of a subnormal child on the family unit." American Journal of Mental Deficiency 61 (July): 210-219.

SCHWARTZ, C. G. (1957) "Perceptions of deviance: wives' definitions of their husbands' mental illness." Psychiatry 20: 275-291.

——— (1956) "The stigma of mental illness." Journal of Rehabilitation 22 (July-August): 7.

SCHWARTZ, M. and S. STRYKER (1970) Deviance, Selves, and Others. Washington, DC: American Sociological Association.

SEARS, R. R. (1970) "Relation of early socialization experiences to self-concept and gender role in middle childhood." Child Development 41 (June): 267-289.

SECORD, R. and S. JOURARD (1953) "The appraisal of bodycathexis and the self." Journal of Consulting Psychology 17: 343-347.

SHELSKY, I. (1957) "The effect of disability on self-concept." Ph.d. dissertation. New York: Columbia University.

SHERE, M. O. (1956) "Socio-emotional factors in families of the twin with cerebral palsy." Exceptional Children 22: 196-199, 206-208.

SHERWOOD, J. J. (1965) "Self-identity and referent others." Sociometry 28 (March): 66-81.

SHIBUTANI, T. (1967) "Reference groups as perspectives," pp. 159-170 in J. G. Manis and B. N. Meltzer (eds.) Symbolic Interaction. Boston, MA: Allyn & Bacon.

SHIRLEY, M. N. (1941) "Impact of mother's personality on the young child." Smith College Studies in Social Work 12: 15-64.

SILVERSTEIN, A. B. and H. A. ROBINSON (1956) "The representation of orthopedic disability in children's figure drawings." Journal of Consulting Psychology 20 (October): 333-341.

SMITS, S. J. (1964) "Reactions of self and others to the obviousness and severity of phsyical disability." Dissertation Abstracts 25: 1-3: 1324-1325.

SOLNIT, A. J. and M. H. STARK (1961) "Mourning and the birth of a defective child." The Psychoanalytic Study of the Child 16: 523-537.

STRAUSS, A. (1962) "Transformations of identity," pp. 63-85 in A. M. Rose (ed.) Human Behavior and Social Processes. Boston, MA: Houghton Mifflin.

STYCOS, J. M. (1955) Family and Fertility in the Lower Class in Puerto Rico. New York: Columbia University Press.

SULLIVAN, H. S. (1947) "The human organism and its necessary environment," pp. 14-27 in Conceptions of Modern Psychiatry. Washington, DC: William Alanson White Psychiatric Foundation.

TEW, B. J., K. M. LAURENCE, H. PAYNE, and K. RAWNSLEY (1977) "Marital stability following the birth of a child with spina bifida." British Journal of Psychiatry 131: 79-82.

THIBAUT, J. (1950) "An experimental study of the cohesion of underprivileged groups." Human Relations 3: 251-278.

TISZA, V. B. (1962) "Management of the parents of the chronically ill child." American Journal of Orthopsychiatry 32 (January): 53-59.

TRICE, H. M. (1970) "The outsider's role in field study," pp. 77-82 in W. J. Filstead (ed.) Qualitative Methodology: Firsthand Involvement With the Social World. Chicago: Markham.

VIDEBECK, R. (1960) "Self-conceptions and the reactions of others." Sociometry 23 (December): 351-359.

VOYSEY, M. (1975) A Constant Burden: The Reconstitution of Family Life. London: Routledge and Kegan Paul.

——— (1972) "Impression management by parents with disabled children." Journal of Health and Social Behavior 13 (March): 80-89.

WALKER, J. H. (1971) "Spina bifida — and the parents." Developmental Medicine and Child Neurology 13: 462-476.

WATERMAN, J. H. (1948) "Psychogenic factors in parental acceptance of feebleminded children." Diseases of the Nervous System 9 (June): 184-187.

WESTLUND, N. and A. Z. PALUMBO (1946) "Parental rejection of crippled children." American Journal of Orthopsychiatry 16 (April): 271-281.

WILKS, J. and E. (1974) Bernard: Bringing Up Our Mongol Son. London: Routledge and Kegan Paul.

WORCHEL, T. L. and P. WORCHEL (1961) "The parental concept of the mentally retarded child." American Journal of Mental Deficiency 65 (May): 782-788.

WORTIS, H. Z. and J. A. MARGOLIES (1955) "Parents of children with cerebral palsy." Medical Social Work 4 (April): 110-120.

WYLIE, R. C. (1974) The Self Concept: A Review of Methodological Considerations and Measuring Instruments. Lincoln, NE: University of Nebraska Press.

WYSOCKI, B. A. and E. WHITNEY (1965) "Body image of crippled children as seen in Draw-A-Person test behavior." Perceptual and Motor Skills 21: 499-504.

ZUNICH, M. and B. E. LEDWITH (1965) "Self-concepts of visually handicapped and sighted children." Perceptual and Motor Skills 21: 771-774.

ZUK, G. H. (1962) "The cultural dilemma and spiritual crisis of the family with a handicapped child." Exceptional Children 28: 405-408.

——— (1959a) "The religious factor and the role of guilt in parental acceptance of the retarded child." American Journal of Mental Deficiency 64 (July): 139-147.

——— (1959b) "Autistic distortions in parents of retarded children." Journal of Consulting Psychology 23 (April): 171-176.

———, R. L. MILLER, J. B. BARTRAM, and F. KLING (1961) "Maternal acceptance of retarded children: a questionnaire study of atttiudes and religious background." Child Development 32: 525-540.

ABOUT THE AUTHOR

Rosalyn Benjamin Darling was born and raised in New York City. She graduated from City College of the City University of New York with a degree in sociology. Subsequently, she received her M.A. and Ph.D. degrees in sociology from The University of Connecticut. While at The University of Connecticut, she held a U.S. Public Health Service Training Fellowship in Medical Sociology.

Dr. Darling taught sociology for seven years at Central Connecticut State College before moving to Johnstown, Pennsylvania in 1977. She currently resides in Johnstown with her husband, Jon (who is also a sociologist), and two sons, Eric Jacob and Seth Benjamin. She teaches courses in the Health-Related Professions Program at the University of Pittsburgh at Johnstown and is Research Director for the Laurel Highlands Hospice. She has published an article on the right to life of severely deformed infants and is currently working on a text book for health professionals on social aspects of birth defects.